WORDS OF LIFE

WORDS *of* LIFE

*Celebrating Fifty Years of the Hesburgh Library's
Message, Mural, and Meaning*

By BILL SCHMITT

Foreword by Theodore Hesburgh, C.S.C.

University of Notre Dame Press · *Notre Dame, Indiana*

Library of Congress Cataloging-in-Publication Data

Schmitt, Bill.
    Words of life : celebrating 50 years of the Hesburgh Library's message, mural, and meaning / by Bill Schmitt ;
foreword by Theodore Hesburgh, C.S.C.
        pages   cm
    ISBN 978-0-268-01783-5 (pbk.) — ISBN 0-268-01783-2 (pbk.)
    1. University of Notre Dame. Library—History.   2. Academic libraries—Indiana—Notre Dame—History.
3. Library architecture—Indiana—Notre Dame.   4. Decoration and ornament, Architectural—Indiana—Notre
Dame.   I. Title.
    Z733.U865S36   2013
    027.7772'89—dc23
                                    2013019562

∞ *The paper in this book meets the guidelines for permanence and durability of the Committee on Production Guidelines for Book Longevity of the Council on Library Resources.*

Contents

Foreword

By their very nature, libraries deal with legacies. And, by their nature, legacies deal with the past and the future. I am grateful that the building we called the Memorial Library in 1963 has reached an important milestone—a fiftieth anniversary—in its mission to help build a better future. And I am glad that this book celebrating the anniversary keeps an eye on tomorrow's information world while also highlighting many wonderful memories that are evoked by the Library and insights from the past that are treasured within its high, strong walls.

Parts of this book evoked happy memories for me, but I choose not to think in terms of any personal legacies or private nostalgia. The love I feel for this Library is an ongoing, present-day love, rich enough to keep me coming back to my office here seven days a week—for as long as the Lord allows me to do so. It is a love of the relationships I am blessed to begin, maintain, and deepen here, and it is a love of the pursuit of information I am blessed to continue here, as students read the news to me and remarkable people from on and off campus visit me to share their thoughts and their prayers. They are interested in lessons I have learned from my experiences in many roles, certainly as president of Our Lady's University, and as a priest—my most cherished role.

The lessons I hope will be drawn from the story of this Library and from my role in its fifty-years-and-counting lifespan are a mixture of past, present, and future. I wanted in 1963, and still desire today, for the Memorial Library literally to stand for the future of Notre Dame as a place of unmatched intellectual achievement, free inquiry, and providential contributions to mankind. But I wanted, and still desire, that this be in the context of a distinctive pursuit of truth that is recognized in the Basilica of the Sacred Heart and in Our Lady atop the Golden Dome. The muralist Millard Sheets captured this pursuit in the Library's *Word of Life* mural, too, showing that the pursuit is a legacy passed along since the dawn of human history, a legacy that has generated countless treasures of wisdom, many of which are preserved and accessible here.

For me and for many in the Notre Dame family, the pursuit of wisdom points to Christ the Teacher, pictured in the mural. But it also begins anew every day with Christ as both Alpha and Omega (as symbolized in a gold etching outside the Library), and with the Holy Spirit, who leads our procession into the future if we are receptive, in all our diversity and incompleteness, to be formed and informed. Let the Library be a place on this campus where that hunger for truth will keep getting stronger, supporting freedom and justice around the world, inspiring excellence, and prodding us to bigger dreams. Let this story of the Library encourage us to celebrate our Notre Dame goal, a legacy that really does bring life, sweetness, and hope.

Theodore Hesburgh, C.S.C.

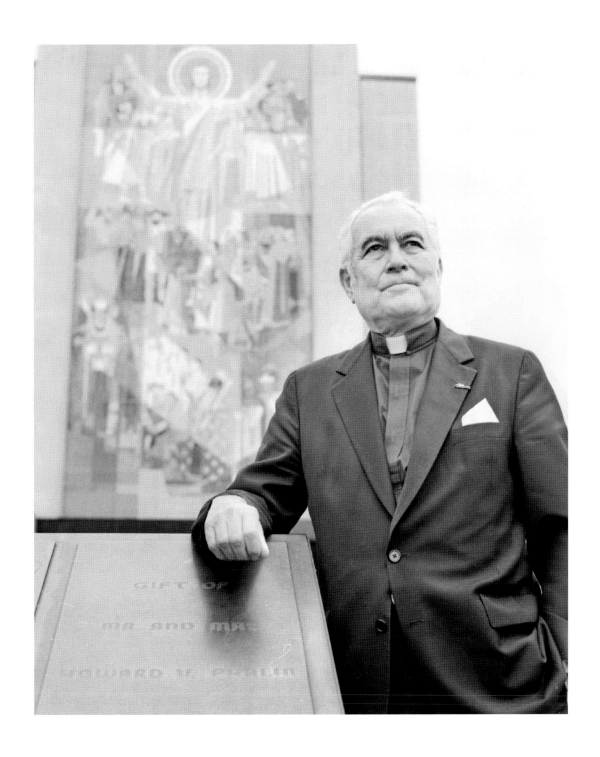

GIFT OF
MR. AND MRS.
HOWARD V. PHALIN

Acknowledgments

The prospect of doing library research often conjures up images of knowledgeable, helpful individuals who will be happy to share information with you, if you'll only ask. In the course of my particular library research—collecting information for this book about the Hesburgh Library—such images proved to be a providential reality. I asked a lot of questions and made many requests for assistance, and these became opportunities to encounter all sorts of remarkable people with kind hearts and great insights.

My gratitude goes out to all those whom I interviewed, all who aided my search for facts, all who helped me check and improve my work, and all who supported me in varied ways during this journey as author. I was privileged to meet many new friends, to deepen many existing friendships, and to draw still closer to the Notre Dame family through their memories and aspirations. Every insight I gained into this great university's past, present, and future made me better, I hope, at my work as one of the communications staff members telling the stories of this place to the world. My endeavors for this book reaffirmed how the Holy Spirit is at work here, making and enriching connections among people, places, symbols, events, traditions—anything offered up for the greater good.

The first of my particular thank-you notes goes to a Stradivarius among instruments of the Holy Spirit, the Reverend Theodore M. Hesburgh, C.S.C., Notre Dame's president emeritus. Throughout the process of my research and writing, Father Ted (as I refer to him in this book) made himself available for interviews and discussions, but even more meaningful has been receiving his blessing, joining him in prayer in his private chapel, and enjoying the hospitality of his office suite on the Library's thirteenth floor. That hospitality, graciously extended and amplified by his assistant, Melanie Chapleau, allowed me to glimpse the way in which Father Ted himself feels at home in the Library—and wants everyone else to feel that way, too.

Numerous people with offices in the Library generously offered me their time and knowledge so I could better describe the place they understand in depth. My thanks go out to all of them, including Diane Parr Walker, the Edward H. Arnold University Librarian, who set the tone of support that greeted me all around the building. Art librarian Marsha Stevenson, along with her coauthors in the excellent Hesburgh Libraries' history *What Is Written Remains,* set a high standard of research for which I am indebted; I appreciated her review of my draft text.

I am grateful to two people with library ties who were crucial in launching this project with me aboard. Professor Susan C. Ohmer, who holds the William Carey and Helen Kuhn Carey Chair in Modern Communication and serves the University as Digital Media Program Manager, believed in me based on my earlier work for the Library and for the University of Notre Dame Press. Katharina Blackstead, who retired in 2012 as advancement officer for the Hesburgh Libraries after nearly forty years on the library faculty, has been a particularly valued friend, supporter, and editor. It was my pleasure to work under her supervision on the *Access* newsletter that covered people and trends of the libraries. The attentiveness to detail that made her an ideal leader for that newsletter and the attentiveness to people that energized her relationships with benefactors combined to make her an invaluable source of guidance and encouragement for me.

Knowing the importance of so many Library officials (including former directors and university librarians) who laid the groundwork for the stories I'm telling here, and knowing the importance of countless benefactors who were vital to the birth and life of the Library, I apologize to all those leaders and supporters who do not receive credit by name in this book. Please know that I take their roles to heart and hope that readers of this book will go beyond these pages (to resources like *What Is Written Remains*) to learn more about the people of the Hesburgh Libraries.

As I go beyond the Library walls in these acknowledgments, I turn with particular gratitude to Mary C. Young, who made valuable contributions as a research assistant. Mary was a Notre Dame graduate student who received her master's degree in early Christian studies in 2012. She found enough spare time away from her curricular activities—many of them firmly grounded in the Hesburgh Library—to generate rich discoveries and enlightening ideas for this book. At the time of this writing, she was working in New York as a researcher and preparing to apply for doctoral studies; any school would be blessed to add her research talents and intellectual enthusiasm to its community.

The university at large served up amazing resources for my work, as usual. I'm primarily speaking of administrators, faculty, and staff of today and yesterday who gave interviews, offered guidance, and provided materials for the book. I thank them for their time and engagement with the process. Chief among these sources of wisdom was senior archivist Peter Lysy. This book gained much from his readiness to be a sherpa amid the verbal content of the University Archives, along with the help of Charles Lamb, assistant director of the Archives, in navigating through the archived images.

Through the archives and other channels, I benefited greatly from the publications and records generated by writers, photographers, and others in the university's offices of development and communications. Reportage by students, too, in university publications such as the *Scholastic* magazine, provided eyewitness accounts from the past. In a number of cases where only periodical titles or press releases or websites are cited, some highly skilled scribes may go unnamed. All these individuals should know my gratitude for their service as communicators on behalf of Notre Dame, a service in which I am privileged to share. Please forgive any instances where appropriate attributions were accidentally excluded or misstated as I attempted to combine an array of sources, from the university and beyond, into a conversational narrative. I have attempted to give proper credit to those who provided nuggets and comprehensive treatments alike. In the latter category, I think particularly of architectural historian Margaret Grubiak's 2010 scholarly article, "Visualizing

the Modern Catholic University: The Original Intention of 'Touchdown Jesus' at the University of Notre Dame," in the journal *Material Religion*—an abundance of insights that deserve to be savored by those who enjoy this book. Among other off-campus sources providing facts or showing support pertinent to this story, I'm thankful to individuals at the *South Bend Tribune;* they led me to an enjoyable conversation with their sports editor emeritus, Joe Doyle of the class of 1949. Also, it was a delight to enjoy the insights and support of Rev. Carolyn Sheets Owen-Towle, the daughter of muralist Millard Sheets; her perspectives on her father's amazing work were unique and uplifting.

One other essential resource within the Notre Dame family is the community of priests in the Congregation of Holy Cross. Members of that community have contributed knowledge and wisdom to projects during all ten years of my work as a university communicator. For this book, besides the most crucial input from Father Ted, I want to thank Rev. Thomas Blantz, C.S.C.; Rev. Paul Doyle, C.S.C.; Rev. Bill Miscamble, C.S.C.; and Rev. Bob Pelton, C.S.C.

I am thankful to the Alliance for Catholic Education (ACE) and the Institute for Educational Initiatives (IEI), the organizations I serve every day as a Notre Dame communicator. Director Rev. Timothy Scully, C.S.C., and associate director Packy Lyden of the IEI have shown special support for my desire to portray the education of both minds and hearts at the University of Notre Dame. Thanks also to esteemed campus friends including Prof. Kevin Christiano, Matt Cashore, Harv Humphrey, and John Nagy.

My wife, Eileen, deserves endless thanks for the support she has shown me throughout this whole journey, which has occupied time during weekends and vacation days. I send my gratitude and love to her and to my daughter, Mary. They represent in my life the ever-present gift for which I reserve the highest thanks and praise. Here I'm thinking of the gift of God's love and the instruction of Christ the Teacher through good times and bad. It has been a privilege to learn about the Hesburgh Library as a place where the Word of Life—and words of life I've shared with people like those cited above—can be celebrated in countless connections. May this book, in some small way, enrich that celebration and expand those connections.

INTRODUCTION

A Moment for Coming Together

"The record surely will note that May 7, 1964, was one of the proudest days in the history of the University of Notre Dame," said the *South Bend Tribune* in an editorial published on that date. "For today the great new library which dominates the campus was dedicated—a dream come true."

Appropriate words, because the dream has much to do with the pursuit of truth through the conveying of wisdom, the convergence of resources, and the convening of community. The events held to dedicate the University of Notre Dame's Memorial Library brought all of those elements to life.

The celebrations, which actually began on May 6, also reflected a moment in history when many people were inclined to come together to imagine new possibilities—to explore their similarities and differences, their strengths and their weaknesses, their frontier enthusiasm and their precipice anxiety. On these two particular days, Notre Dame was privileged to be the common ground where leaders from various segments of American society and the Roman Catholic Church could join together to contemplate both accomplishments and the implications of those accomplishments.

The two days of events, spanning prayer, punditry, pomp, and simple pleasure, allowed Notre Dame once again to play its role of bringing hope. The building at the center of the action still stands tall today—a beloved landmark, a reminder of the joys of coming together, an invitation to imagine even as one grounds oneself.

"It was a very nice day, a sunny day," recalls John Marszalek, '63 M.A., '68 Ph.D., who joined the thousands sitting in chairs that had been "jammed in" between the Library's reflecting pool and Notre Dame Stadium for the May 7 dedication ceremonies. "I remember thinking what an incredible day it was"—partly thanks to his personal optimism that the new Library promised more study space and more comfort for history graduate students such as him.

TAKING THE DEDICATION VERY PERSONALLY

Before the dedication day itself, students of history and the future were invited to a related event, a "Symposium on the Person in the Contemporary World," held in the Library's new auditorium on May 6. Notre Dame had invited top scholars from various disciplines to make sense of that compelling period in American and world affairs called the '60s—a time when concerns driven by the Cold War and other challenges intermingled with a sense of wonder about stunning opportunities.

The church was welcomed wholeheartedly into this experience of wonderment. On May 7, Ascension Thursday, a Solemn Pontifical Mass and a blessing of the "world's largest college library building" attracted a congregation that newspaper accounts estimated at 3,000–4,000 people. No fewer than three cardinals participated. Even Pope Paul VI, who had received an honorary degree from Notre Dame in 1960 as Giovanni Battista Cardinal Montini, sent a message of blessing to the university community and to his "beloved son," Rev. Theodore M. Hesburgh, C.S.C. Father Hesburgh—referred to in this book as Father Ted—had envisioned the celebration and its celebrants, and had initiated the whole cause for joy.

Influential leaders of academia and public affairs were part of the scene, too. An outdoor academic convocation and an evening banquet welcomed the president of Columbia University and the chancellor of Indiana University as featured speakers, among many others. Some twenty-five honorary degrees were conferred. The program for the day's events lists Rev. Edmund P. Joyce, C.S.C., the university's executive vice president and Father Ted's close assistant and confidant in many matters (including the construction of the Library), as the General Chairman for the Dedication.

The most visually dramatic element of the dedication events was the 134-foot-high mural, titled *The Word of Life* but later known more widely as "Touchdown Jesus." All those gathered in their folding chairs for the May 7 outdoor ceremonies looked up at the mammoth mural from the new Library Quad. An official unveiling had been scheduled to take place on the morning of May 7, but, days before, strong winds had torn away the canvas curtain behind which the mural's complicated installation had occurred. The granite Jesus, with hands outstretched,

3

4

rose thirteen stories above the platform that served as altar in the morning and convocation stage in the afternoon.

Memorial Library, whose name was changed to the Rev. Theodore M. Hesburgh Library in 1987 upon Father Ted's retirement after thirty-five years as university president, was launched in style with those dedication events.

The building actually had opened for business on September 18, 1963, at the start of the 1963–64 academic year, so as to maintain student and faculty access to the roughly 500,000 volumes that had been transferred from the previous University Library (today known as Bond Hall). Memorial Library's theme-rich dedication in 1964 was crucial in making this fourteen-story building (thirteen stories plus a penthouse), with a footprint covering about two acres and an official capacity of two million books, a vivid part of Notre Dame's character, mission, and tradition. Nevertheless, its opening one year earlier injected it immediately into the daily flow of university life.

Now fifty years old, this building that was originally called Memorial Library in tribute to more than 23,000 individual and institutional benefactors, is central in telling countless stories about the daily life and the deeper vision of Notre Dame. Perhaps the quintessential story of that vision is the "trilogy" of focal points on campus so often described by Father Ted, testifying to his love of the building—a love inseparable from his love for the university. When you look out upon the university from downtown South Bend, "you see three things. You see the spire of the church—it's a Catholic university; you see Our Lady on the dome—it's the University of Our Lady; and you see the Library—the center of the intellectual life. And that's the vision of Notre Dame," Father Ted recalled in a 2011 interview.

That's just the beginning. Stories about the building's past, present, and future—about its architectural novelty on campus, its *Word of Life* mural, and more—shed light on Father Ted himself, on his vision for the university in the 1960s, and on the Notre Dame identity dating from its founding by Rev. Edward Sorin, C.S.C., through to today. These are stories about Notre Dame's identity and its conviction that faith and reason, modernity and religion, the secular and the sacred, can and must go together.

They're stories about convergence, continuity, and community. They're enduring stories about big dreams and bold faith, as expressed in the inaugural speech of University President Rev. John Jenkins, C.S.C., in 2005. Echoing Father Sorin's determination not only to rebuild the Main Building destroyed by fire in 1879, but to make it larger and grander, Father Jenkins called for the twenty-first-century Notre Dame to be "one of the preeminent research institutions in the world, a center for learning whose intellectual and religious traditions converge to make it a healing, unifying, enlightening force for a world deeply in need." He concluded, "Let no one ever again say that we dreamed too small."

The Hesburgh Library, in some ways very much a product of the 1960s, expresses a kind of continuity between the aspirations of Sorin and Jenkins. At all three points in the timeline, being different was inseparable from making a difference—and bold dreams were an inevitable response to times of uncertainty, need, and opportunity.

REASON FOR ANXIETY, ROOM FOR HOPE

The May 6, 1964, symposium that served as the prelude to the dedication of the Memorial Library affirmed that Notre Dame could make a difference—and make news—by casting a scholarly, caring eye on the state of humankind.

"Four of the world's leading scholars addressed themselves today to the problem of the individual in the contemporary world at dedication ceremonies for Notre Dame University's new

13-story, $8-million library, said to be the largest university library building in the world," reported Frank Hughes in the *Chicago Tribune*. Under the headline, "'Man' is Topic at Notre Dame," Hughes said "a psychiatrist, a theologian, a scientist, and a philosopher" had come together to assess how, in the eyes of one of the speakers, "man has been brought face to face with the fundamental shortcomings of his own character."

According to Hughes, psychiatrist Dana Farnsworth, a professor and director of health services at Harvard University, cautioned that modern man was coming to expect (unrealistically) that everything is possible, while also suffering a sense of "surfeit and boredom from massive dissemination of ideas, many of them not worth transmitting."

The whole purpose of the symposium was to focus on the really big ideas that could guide humanity in discerning between the possible and the desirable. A wide range of United States opinion makers, including journalists, paid attention because they had begun to see Notre Dame as a place where such ideas—and the information to support them—were being nurtured in distinctive ways. A February 9, 1962, issue of *Time* magazine featuring Father Ted on the cover had helped spread awareness, but interest in this university-on-the-move had been growing since the 1950s.

The symposium's two designated leaders reflected the breadth of Notre Dame's reach. Doctor Kenneth Thompson, a scholar of international relations and vice president of the Rockefeller Foundation, served as chairman and interlocutor with the panelists. Meanwhile, the honorary chairman presiding at the day's event was no less an ecclesial luminary than Eugene Cardinal Tisserant, dean of the Sacred College of Cardinals and prefect of the Vatican Library.

Father Ted offered opening remarks, asserting society's zeitgeist of opportunity and uncertainty: "The theme of this conference is the human person—his estrangement and alienation in today's world, but also his inner dignity and enduring hope for a better tomorrow." (These and other remarks from the symposium are found in a transcript, *The Person in Contemporary Society*, published and preserved today on the Hesburgh Library's shelves.)

The negativism so often evinced in the culture of the time could not provide sustenance, he went on. "Over and above the pessimistic vision is the challenge to greatness that still confronts every person—even modern man. He can whine, moan, or rebel, but he can also rise above all of this and create in these our times, despite all the temptations of impersonal anonymity or defeatism, a new vision of the person who knows and accepts himself and rises above all inhuman obstacles to contribute to a new world that is sublimely personal and creative."

Thompson thanked Notre Dame for sharing "the remarkable originality and creativity of your great President." He said, "You have moved forward in higher education in recent months and years as few universities anywhere in the world."

TWENTY-FIVE CENTS

FEBRUARY 9, 1962

"Where are the Catholic intellectuals?"

TIME

WSMAGAZINE

NOTRE DAME'S
PRESIDENT
HESBURGH

HENRY KOERNER

$7.00 A YEAR   (REG. U.S. PAT. OFF.)   VOL. LXXIX NO. 6

The first of the four symposium speakers was Rev. Louis Bouyer, a French theologian at the Institut Catholique de Paris, consultant to the Vatican, and faculty member in Notre Dame's liturgy program. He acknowledged the coexistence of optimism and angst in the atmosphere of 1964. "In spite of that, I should be inclined to think that the Christian faith, just because it enables us to see more deeply and more clearly into the entangled lines of man's history, can bring to us the sole realistic possibility of finding a positive and constructive way between naïve and chimeric optimism and any kind of paralyzing pessimism."

He noted "the impression so common today that we are entering a new era, and even that a mutation of the whole outlook and life of man has now begun." He saw great hope in an emerging global consciousness and in a stampede of new information. "Here lies the greatest paradox in the situation of modern man: that to any individual mind, even that of the best scholar, the difficulty of not remaining provincial when he tries to be universal is greater than it has ever been." But at least we are not reliant on imagination alone, he added; we can be rooted in reality because we receive a growing abundance of facts from around the world.

This was a summons to community and collaboration across disciplines because "we are either to cease to think at all, or we are to think together. . . . The scientist, the historian, the psychologist, the moral philosopher, and the religious thinker must function not any longer in a spirit of antagonism but in a spirit of mutual enlightenment and necessary collaboration, if all these men intend to be not only specialists, but real and complete men, and specialists only for the general benefit of mankind."

Thompson pointed out that modern communications technology made the human mission of service more intense and daunting. He cited a lesson from the history of international relations. "If one reads the papers of Secretary of State Thomas Jefferson, one finds him writing to a friend saying that for nearly two years no word had come from the Consul General in Madrid. He goes on that, if in the following year nothing is heard, he would plan to do something about it." This stands in sharp contrast with the life of the modern 1964 diplomat, Thompson pointed out: "In an era of trip-hammer diplomacy, the intensification of communication heightens even more the urgency of discovering deeper forms of community among mankind."

The moral philosopher, John E. Smith, chairman of the Department of Philosophy at Yale, commented how essential it is to understand what it means to be human at a time when the world is struggling with issues of human equality, human rights, and human freedom. He observed, "There is little point in the demand for the acknowledgment of human dignity and the equality of persons if we do not know what we mean by a person."

Hugh Stott Taylor, a renowned chemist at Princeton University who years earlier had helped establish the Catholic chaplaincy there, restated Father Ted's remarks at the California Institute of Technology in 1963: "Ours is a time of great change, of revolutionary winds, of new breakthroughs on every front. . . . Should the one great problem, the condition of man, be deprived of breakthroughs in our times? . . . Should we pioneer in space and be timid on earth? . . . Must we break the bonds of earth and leave man in bondage below?" These questions from Hesburgh were a call for collaboration and cooperation among "all men of good will" to seek answers to all the great questions.

None of these reflections could be dismissed as academic rhetoric irrelevant to the practical concerns of the times. Less than two months after the Memorial Library dedication, Father Ted would be linking his arms with Dr. Martin Luther King and singing "We Shall Overcome" at a massive civil rights rally in Chicago.

VOICES FROM LOFTY LEVELS

After serving as honorary chairman for the symposium, Cardinal Tisserant took the role of principal celebrant at the Solemn Pontifical Mass—a highpoint for the morning of the Feast of the Ascension. The sermon was delivered by Albert Cardinal Meyer, who headed the then-largest Catholic diocese in the United States as archbishop of Chicago.

These two princes of the church were upstaged, one might say, by Pope Paul VI himself. Although not physically present, the pope provided a written message in which he spoke as an honorary alumnus of Notre Dame: "Recalling the happy memory of Our visit to your University, beloved son, and the honorary doctorate by which We became an alumnus, We gladly send you Our greetings and felicitations on the dedication of the new Memorial Library at Notre Dame."

"We pray that this additional repository of wisdom and knowledge may serve as a valuable instrument in the pursuit of truth and the defense and development of faith," the pontiff continued. He affirmed that "the quest for truth requires freedom" while also citing the need for charity, justice, human dignity—and the duty of Catholic professors and students to respect church teachings in faith and morals—as complements to science and freedom. He prayed that the new Memorial Library "will contribute richly to the advancement of truth."

There was a third cardinal on campus that day, as reported by *Notre Dame,* a magazine published during those years by the Notre Dame Foundation and the university's development office. Joseph Cardinal Ritter, archbishop of St. Louis, performed the blessing of the Library building later in the afternoon. Ritter's plea to God at that time resonates still today: "Kindly bless and sanctify this Library constructed to collect, preserve, and make available divine and human knowledge contained in books, records, and documents. Aid its continued increase in volumes and in depth of wisdom. May it safely withstand fire, wind, and buffets of damaging elements, and preserve its wealth from destruction by man or time."

Ritter went on to invoke the Holy Spirit's gifts upon seekers of wisdom and truth, as well as those "who mine new treasures by ever advancing methods of research. May they grow in justice, peace, and in love so that the word spoken and written in time may find fulfillment in truth eternal."

All three cardinals were, by dint of their office, participating in the Second Vatican Council, the momentous gathering of church leaders that took place between 1962 and 1965. Cardinal Meyer, in his Pontifical Mass homily, reflected on the importance of seeking truth. He noted that truth itself does not change but the human drama is one of drawing closer to it and viewing it from "continually changing" perspectives.

"The renewal which is the expressed objective of the Second Vatican Council is not in the truth itself, which we have in the Word of Life," Meyer said, "but in our more perfect possession of it, our wider interpretation of it, our fuller living of it."

He offered a bit of explanation for the title of the granite mural, *The Word of Life,* which soared above the platform where he was speaking. The term is used at the start of an Epistle, in 1 John 1:1, which Meyer proceeded to read: "That which was from the beginning, which we have heard, which we have seen with our eyes, which we have looked at and our hands have touched—this we proclaim concerning 'The Word of Life.'"

The Word of Life, Meyer said, "is our Savior, Jesus Christ." Christ is called the Word "because He is God's utterance—the image of the invisible God." Christ "has become for us God-given wisdom," Meyer said. "All the words of men, if they are true words, reflect and reproduce the riches of the one eternal Word of Life." He added that Christ is also called the Life "because He came into the world and lived and died for us to give us eternal life."

Cardinal Meyer foresaw great fruitfulness to be borne in the intellectual community, "the family of scholars," when it demonstrates love, communion, and fellowship—"when the whole family is at one in the common search for truth."

For the second consecutive day, journalists were on hand to capture the scene. "The red velvet thrones of three cardinals, princes of the church, flanked the altar set up beneath clear blue skies on the mall," wrote Frank Hughes for the *Chicago Tribune* and other newspapers.

Roger Birdsell reported that morning in the *South Bend Tribune,* "The Notre Dame Band played the processional, and the student chorus joined the seminary choir for the recessional." He added, "The flower-banked, red and white outdoor altar was placed between the reflecting pool and the [Library] building, and was to be converted to a stage this afternoon for the dedicatory convocation." Birdsell also noted that Father Edmund Joyce, in his remarks, expressed the hope that students "may raise their hearts and minds to Christ the Teacher."

FORESIGHT FROM THE GRASS ROOTS

Then–graduate student John Marszalek recalls that the crowded outdoor convocation he attended that day did feel like an academic family gathering. Marszalek, interviewed for this book in 2012, is executive director of the Ulysses S. Grant Presidential Library and Giles Distinguished Professor Emeritus of History at Mississippi State University. "There was a bunch of us graduate students there" to share in the excitement, he says of the convocation.

The towering figure of *The Word of Life*, represented as Christ the Teacher, the alpha and omega for an unbroken pursuit of wisdom represented by numerous figures through history, could not be missed as the centerpiece—a great high priest for a community of educated minds and hearts. Was this symbolic meaning of the design and of the day's events a striking part of Marszalek's experience as he sat in the vast expanse of folding chairs? No, he acknowledges. "The religious side was almost taken for granted," he recalls. "I don't remember much conversation about it." Of course, there was discussion about the building itself. It had received its share of criticism for its large and nonconforming dimensions, but the mural's Catholic message seemed to have no vocal detractors.

That's not to say *The Word of Life* struck his friends as unremarkable. "It was a work of art and an engineering phenomenon," admired for the work that had gone into it, not to mention the dozens of kinds (and at least 6,000 pieces) of granite that literally had gone into it—after being identified and selected from all over the world, as well as shaped and positioned with immense creativity and craftsmanship. "People were really impressed from that point of view—how do you put together something as intricate as that?"

Having begun his Notre Dame studies in 1961, Marszalek was also conscious that the Memorial Library was giving new shape to other things, too. The space where he sat for the convocation, between the Library and the stadium, was the university's newest quad, a zone of modernity particularly focused on research and science, already birthing such buildings as the Information Technology Center and the Radiation Research Building.

North of Notre Dame Stadium, this land had opened up with the potential for additional buildings. Landmarks from Notre Dame's past—such as Vetville, where Father Ted had once served as a chaplain to the families of World War II veterans attending college on the G.I. Bill, and Cartier Field, which was the original venue for football on campus before Notre Dame Stadium existed—had disappeared so that the Library could generate its sense of new possibilities.

"The campus just got so much bigger, as it seemed to us," says Marszalek. "You were opening a whole area of campus."

The transformation left room for both enthusiasm and sarcasm. While the enthusiasm prompted thoughts about new campus buildings and more modern designs, the sarcasm focused on whether Father Ted had chosen to tear up Cartier Field out of disdain for the Fighting Irish football team, which recently had been performing poorly in the pre-Parseghian days. (The Parseghian era started in the fall of 1964.) The Library's towering shape also prompted some to see Father Ted's disdain expressed in other ways. "The story went that the Library cast its shadow on the football field." Marszalek says that he and many other graduate students dismissed such football-centric small talk. (Other sources have confirmed that Father Ted actually likes football—including Notre Dame football, so long as the athletics are in tandem with academic accomplishment.) Instead, these budding scholars "were ecstatic about the new Library and what it meant to those of us who would soon graduate from Notre Dame and would graduate in the future."

Even at its dedication, the Memorial Library was serving as a crossroads for divergent perspectives and possibilities, a place capturing meaning from the past, present, and future. For Marszalek and many like him who gathered on those two days of celebration, the experience could be summed up as one of change and pride for Notre Dame: "What it said about the institution and what it did for the institution—both the symbolism and the real impact it had—are crucial in the history of the university."

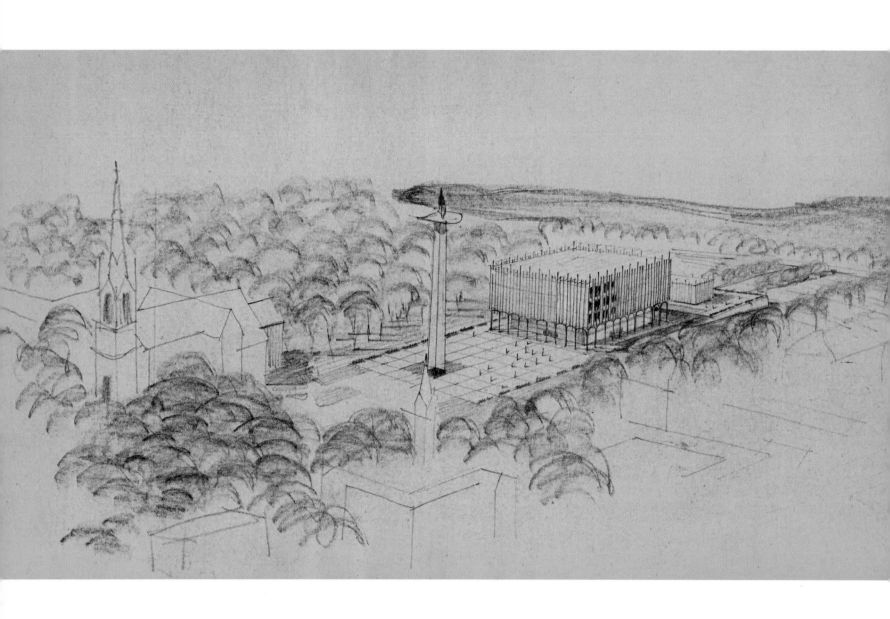

Chapter One
DESIGNING WISDOM

In keeping with the maxim, one might say that the "invention" of the Memorial Library in the 1960s definitely had necessity as its mother. But, with his knack for marrying the needs of the moment to an enduring sense of purpose, Rev. Theodore Hesburgh, C.S.C., was unmistakably the father.

WHEN CHANGE IS OVERDUE

The necessity for the project came in the form of overcrowding and unmet expectations at the University Library that had served Notre Dame since 1917. The stately Renaissance-style building that today is called Bond Hall was the home of approximately 400,000 volumes by the mid-1950s and was drawing criticism, not so much because it couldn't hold the books but because it could not simultaneously meet the demands of a 400 percent larger student population, the evolving expectations for libraries of the day, and the growing aspirations for the university of tomorrow.

Not only had Notre Dame changed, but the expert wisdom about the proper design of a library had changed "dramatically" in the forty years following construction of the University Library, says Marsha Stevenson in *What is Written Remains: Historical Essays on the Libraries of Notre Dame.* (The 1994 essay by Stevenson, current art librarian and former head of the reference department, provided a number of details—about both the older and newer libraries—for this book.)

The $250,000 building that was dedicated at the university's diamond jubilee ceremonies in April 1917 was seen at the time as a splendid new home for the collection of about 100,000 books that previously had been housed on the third floor of the Main Building. These books constituted the Lemonnier Library, named for Rev. Augustus Lemonnier, C.S.C., the Holy Cross priest (and nephew of Notre Dame founder Rev. Edward Sorin, C.S.C.) who had overseen Notre Dame's establishment of a lending library. He was president of Notre Dame from 1872 to his death in 1874, just several years before the 1879 Main Building fire destroyed the 10,000 books that had been assembled up to that time.

The post-fire collection was still called the Lemonnier Library well into the twentieth century. "That was the official title, but nobody knew that, I think," recalls Rev. Tom Blantz, C.S.C., professor of history and former director of the University Archives. As a result, the library's 1917-vintage home was generally called the University Library.

A *South Bend Tribune* story in 1916 reported that the new library under construction at that time would have two large reading rooms and a reference room, plus working rooms, along with an ample area set aside for the rapidly proliferating media of the time—newspapers and magazines. This was especially appropriate at Notre Dame to accommodate the university's new school of journalism. The building also would have room for the University Archives and an art collection.

For the most part, books were stored efficiently and massively in "closed stacks," separate from the large, centralized spaces where the students and faculty would sit down and read. Hand delivery to patrons was deemed one of the modern conveniences of the day. But, as Stevenson explains, the efficiencies of 1917 lost much of their appeal over time. "In the 1940s, it became popular to subdivide main libraries" into separate subject categories. Library designers increasingly shunned large, all-purpose reading rooms and favored smaller, quieter spaces, where patrons could interact directly with books in open stacks, grouped by their areas of interest.

An assessment of the University Library in the early 1950s led to numerous modifications, trying to bring a growing number of books nearer to a growing number of students in comfortable and convenient settings. Notre Dame also tackled the existing space challenges by moving some books to other facilities on campus. The Nieuwland Library for chemistry, physics, and mathematics had opened in 1953. A *South Bend Tribune* article in 1960 reported that the University Library was home to 472,000 volumes, with specialized libraries housing 200,000 more. Today, the "Hesburgh Libraries" are very much a plural phenomenon; they comprise, in addition to the flagship building, eight additional libraries and information centers around campus. (That tally also does not include the Kresge Law Library, which is independent, under the auspices of the Notre Dame Law School.)

In spite of the adaptations to library trends in the 1950s, "it became increasingly apparent that construction of a new building was inevitable," says Stevenson. "The changing philosophy of

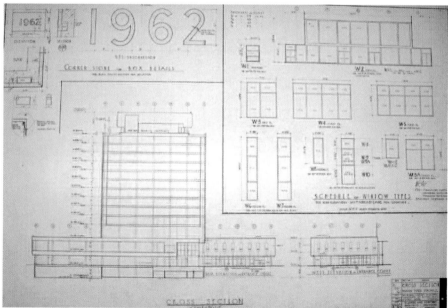

library service that emphasized the juxtaposition of readers and books had created a conflict between form and function that could not be resolved within the confines of the 1917 structure."

There were other types of conflict, too. Maureen Gleason, who was a general reference librarian in the University Library in the late 1950s before rising to deputy director of the next-generation university libraries in the 1990s, recalls that the old building had become unpopular with many users. "It was deteriorating badly and very, very much overcrowded," she said in a 2011 interview.

"That was a miserable little building," agreed Father Ted in a separate interview, referring to the University Library prior to its reincarnation as the School of Architecture, later refurbished again and renamed Bond Hall.

To Father Ted, his conflict with the old library was less about its recalling the past and more about its forestalling the future. Ever since his inauguration as president of the University of Notre Dame in 1952, at the age of thirty-five, he had been talking about the need for a new library. In his first interview with the *Notre Dame* development magazine in that year, he had called for "a real working library—one like they have at Princeton."

MARRYING NEED AND PURPOSE

During the 1950s, Father Ted continued to develop and promote his call for a new library. Issues of the *Notre Dame* magazine included a regular "President's Page" feature in which one could see the president's evolving vision of a Catholic university taking on the issues of the modern world, and the need for a library was inseparable from that vision.

In his magazine commentary for the fall of 1957, he spoke of his conviction that a Catholic university could make a distinct difference that no public institution could. "Ours is an apostolate that no secular university today can undertake—for they are largely cut off from a tradition of knowledge which comes only through faith in the mind and faith in God—the highest wisdom of Christian philosophy and Catholic theology. We must be conscious of our past heritage and enthusiastic in bringing new insights of Christian wisdom to the present."

With words that resonate in the remarks of University President Rev. John Jenkins, C.S.C., during his inauguration in 2005, calling for Notre Dame to be different so it can make a difference in the world, Hesburgh's 1957 commentary went on: "Here is a task for the greatest minds and the most devoted hearts and completely dedicated lives. I know of no other place on earth where we might make a better beginning than at Notre Dame, a new center of Christian culture, an awakening of the potential of Christian wisdom, applied to the problems of our age. As a Catholic university we must not fail to exploit the full power of Christian wisdom to order what is disordered, to complete what is good but incomplete, to meet insufficient knowledge with the fullness of truth, to give a new direction and a wider, saner perspective to all that is good and true in our times."

In a "President's Page" from the fall of 1958, Father Ted made the connection between this vision for the university and the vision for a new library. As a busy world traveler precisely because of his engagement with the pressing concerns of the times, he wrote that "I have visited many of the world's famous universities and have seen the libraries created by these universities. May I say that, as I have studied such institutions, a new library for Notre Dame has taken high priority in my dreams for the future."

Elsewhere, he had written, "Great libraries, as you know, exist apart from universities, but no university can ever be great without a great library." But he also made it clear that his aspiration for Notre Dame to be a great institution was inseparable from a fatherly solicitude toward the people of Notre Dame and their own engagement in the world through a great library.

"It must be the place where students of the future will be delighted to spend many hours of every day. There in silence they will meet the best of books from the greatest of minds; there in the quiet by themselves they will carry on the search for knowledge and truth that will change their whole lives."

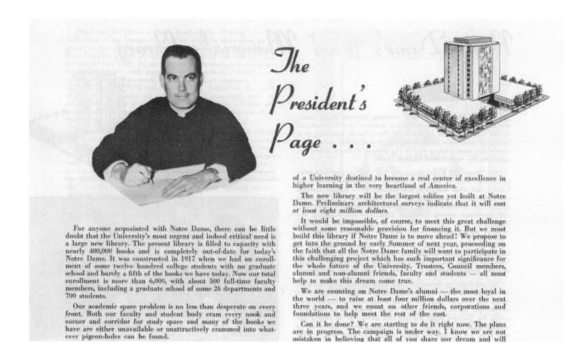

The President's Page . . .

For anyone acquainted with Notre Dame, there can be little doubt that the University's most urgent and indeed critical need is a large new library. The present library is filled to capacity with nearly 400,000 books and is completely out-of-date for today's Notre Dame. It was constructed in 1917 when we had an enrollment of some twelve hundred college students with no graduate school and barely a fifth of the books we have today. Now our total enrollment is more than 6,000, with about 500 full-time faculty members, including a graduate school of some 26 departments and 700 students.

Our academic space problem is no less than desperate on every front. Both our faculty and student body cram every nook and corner and corridor for study space and many of the books we have are either unavailable or unattractively crammed into whatever pigeon-holes can be found.

of a University destined to become a real center of excellence in higher learning in the very heartland of America.

The new library will be the largest edifice yet built at Notre Dame. Preliminary architectural surveys indicate that it will cost *at least eight million dollars.*

It would be impossible, of course, to meet this great challenge without some reasonable provision for financing it. But we must build this library if Notre Dame is to move ahead! We propose to get into the ground by early Summer of next year, proceeding on the faith that all the Notre Dame family will want to participate in this challenging project which has such important significance for the whole future of the University. Trustees, Council members, alumni and non-alumni friends, faculty and students — all must help to make this dream come true.

We are counting on Notre Dame's alumni — the most loyal in the world — to raise at least four million dollars over the next three years, and we count on other friends, corporations and foundations to help meet the rest of the cost.

Can it be done? We are starting to do it right now. The plans are in progress. The campaign is under way. I know we are not mistaken in believing that all of you share our dream and will

Father Ted reaffirmed and expanded this picture of the intellectually engaged student in a spring 1960 "President's Page." He wrote, "Vitally needed is a place where at least half of our students can at any time find a quiet and calm atmosphere, the necessary books, and a pervading spirit of study. A large library with many open stack rooms for study and numerous carrels for graduate students would fill this need in a manner both appropriate and long overdue. A minimal estimate of adequate size would be provision for about 1-1/2 to 2 million books." (He has since talked about his aspiration for a library of 6 million items—an almost uncanny leap in terms of books alone, but both imaginable and achievable given the emergence of new media, from vinyl records and microfilm in the 1960s to DVDs and online/digital products of the twenty-first century. Indeed, that "uncanny" aspiration has essentially been achieved, depending on how one counts titles, online and otherwise.

Father Ted, never inclined to think small or settle for the status quo, dismissed suggestions for an incremental approach to increasing the university's book storage capacity. Simply keeping the old University Library and building enough space to double current capacity "would be looking backwards instead of forward," he wrote in a 1961 "President's Page" feature. "Instead, we say, let's build a library four or five times as big as the present structure. As the library fills with books,

Designing Wisdom

we'll build something else to take care of other needs. Let's look ahead and dream big the way the men who came here years ago dreamed big."

His inclination toward big dreams always seemed to spring from the dual root of intellectual enthusiasm and hope-filled faith. In another "President's Page" from 1961, Father Ted spoke of "a splendid new library that will be a living, working monument to the saints and scholars of all times: those long dead and those who follow them with bright eyes and pure hearts through the portals of Notre Dame in our day."

That hope-filled faith in people and in prospects for the future was inseparable from knowledge of the past, Father Ted pointed out in a 2011 interview. His vision for the Memorial Library, and perhaps to some degree his passion for a place of monumental dimensions, entailed a building that "puts us in touch with the whole history of Christianity, which is 2,000 years old," he said. "Most of that is in print, one way or the other. It's important to have a building in which the whole history is recounted."

With Father Ted shaping and articulating the vision for the library during the 1950s and early 1960s, others were looking more deeply into the details of a plan. What would be the features of the building? Where on campus would it be located? What would be its priorities?

Victor Schaefer, director of the University Library, was a leading figure in planning for the library and in articulating its centrality to the university, its mission, and its stakeholders. It was he who submitted a "Program for the Architect" in mid-December 1959, outlining the call for a new library and clearing the way for detailed planning.

Earlier that year, Schaefer had solicited faculty suggestions about the idea. Then, in a memorandum to Rev. Philip Moore, C.S.C., academic assistant to the president, he had advanced the discussions by outlining the philosophy of a university library. By definition, a library is not merely a building but also a program of strategies and activities, he argued, quoting a document from the University of Iowa's library planning committee. Beyond the building itself, there must be "a comprehensive attempt to place within a building a great number of activities in which the medium of print is necessary to a successful program of action."

"The primary characteristic of a good academic library is its complete identification with its own institution," Schaefer wrote in the memo, adding that "the measure of a library's excellence is the extent to which its services and resources support the institution's objectives and promote student and faculty achievement." Among his own visions for the place, he opposed closed stacks and saw a growing need for easy access to a wider variety of books, partly because universities were moving away from textbook-focused courses and toward independent research requiring original sources.

Father Moore was appointed to chair a faculty planning committee. In a brief letter to the entire faculty at the start of 1960, he wrote, "Assurance can be given that every effort will be made to plan a building which is in accordance with the latest ideas on the functions of a university library and which will meet the needs of Notre Dame for years to come."

PASSING THE PLATE

As the vision for the future became better articulated and needs and opportunities became better aligned during the late 1950s and early 1960s, one other key requirement for birthing the Memorial Library—raising the funds—was revved up.

The gears had been engaged in 1958, when the university announced a $66.6 million development plan spanning ten years. The campaign was called the "Program for the Future," and it included all sorts of goals, including money for faculty salaries, research, and student aid. But about $19 million of the total was targeted for new buildings, with a library slated for $5 million. Other buildings mentioned (in the description from the archived *Notre Dame* development publication for alumni) were a $5 million fieldhouse and a $3.5 million auditorium.

The drive to raise money for a library came into even sharper focus in September 1960, when the Ford Foundation announced its "Special Program in Education," with particular incentives for Notre Dame. The foundation offered Notre Dame (along with four other rapidly improving universities) a grant of $6 million, as reported in Marsha Stevenson's essay. The offer was based on the school's leading-edge achievements to date and its plan for future developments "commensurate in scope, imagination, and practicability to the vast needs of American society."

The only catch was that the grant would be contingent on Notre Dame's ability to raise $12 million over three years from alumni and other benefactors. Father Ted, again defaulting to an even greater dream, responded that Notre Dame would aim to raise not $12 million but $18 million—keeping in mind the overall $66.6 million goal looming later in the decade. This time, relative to the first-step goal of $18 million, the development office listed the Library as the top priority project, with a price tag of $8 million.

Designing Wisdom

The race was on to meet the foundation's deadline, with alumni responding well, famed industrialist J. Peter Grace chairing the campaign, and Father Ted helping to inspire the whole effort. Father Ted was especially enthusiastic when it came to the Library as an urgent cause for giving. In a 1960 fund-raising booklet for the library that actually was prepared before the Ford Foundation announcement, he acknowledged that financing such a project might be a challenge.

"But we must build this library if Notre Dame is to move ahead!" he responded in the booklet. "We propose to get into the ground by early summer of next year, proceeding on the faith that all the Notre Dame family will want to participate in this challenging project, which has such important significance for the whole future of the University. . . . We are counting on Notre Dame's alumni—the most loyal in the world—to raise at least $4 million over the next three years, and we count on other friends, corporations, and foundations to help meet the rest of the cost."

Professor John Frederick, respected chair of the Department of English, expanded the sense of urgency: "In this year of 1960," he wrote in the same booklet, "no thoughtful person can fail

to see that our very civilization can be destroyed by the fruits of knowledge—knowledge unguided by charity and unqualified by reverence. It seems to me terribly clear today that the place of the Christian university in higher education is of crucial importance. That is why I see, literally, no limit to the future greatness of Notre Dame. The new library is certainly an essential step on the road to that greatness."

Father Ted reflected the same zeal in his "President's Page" missives. Construction of the Library had been set to start in 1961 before all the money had been pledged. In his fall 1961 commentary, writing at the time of the startup of construction, he called that period "Notre Dame's moment of truth." He deemed it time to remind his readers of the fight song: "What though the odds be great or small, Old Notre Dame will win over all."

He shared with alumni and benefactors how much his vision was reliant on a leap of faith—in God and in His providential work through people: "Because we need this, we have begun to build it—not with the money in hand, no more than Father Sorin had, but with the same faith

in you and in Notre Dame's future. Whether this spells folly or vision is the substance of our moment of truth this fall. Either the funds mount as the building mounts, or we are in trouble. . . . As I stand beside the gaping two acre excavation for the new Memorial Library, and listen to the pile drivers, hammering in the foundation, I confess to an occasional passing twinge of fear, but not to a lack of confidence in all of you who have helped make Notre Dame the shining beacon that it is today. What Notre Dame will be tomorrow is also in your generous hands to make."

(The zeal, trust in providence, and appreciation for benefactors in relation to construction projects all remain unchanged today, but the "twinge of fear" part of Father Ted's remarks has been addressed with today's updated policy on fund-raising. "We require 100 percent of the money pledged, and three quarters of it in hand, before we start construction on a major new building," says University Architect and Associate Vice President Douglas Marsh.)

Nevertheless, Father Ted's faith bore fruit. A short time after the publication of that article, pledges and contributions toward the "$18 million Challenge" declared by Father Ted passed the $10 million mark, leaving the university far ahead of the pace needed to earn the Ford Foundation money.

In the same issue of the *Notre Dame* development publication where that huge progress was announced, Father Ted continued his fund-raising appeal for the Library, again tying the project to the heart and soul of Notre Dame's mission as a compassionate force in the world. He explained in a commentary that he had returned from an international trip where he had been deeply affected by such widespread problems as hunger.

"When you tighten your belts and give a sacrificial gift to the new Library, you should understand that what will happen in this Library will in some small measure affect the world and all of its problems," he wrote. "I don't mean that Notre Dame is going to solve all the world's problems, but I am convinced that many of our students who pass through the doors of this Library are going to comprehend better just what the whole world is today, and what it needs. Some of them are going to respond to these needs, and are going to help people in far-off lands find some of the answers they need."

The alumni and friends of Notre Dame came through as they always do. As a result of the challenge to raise $18 million by June 30, 1963, Notre Dame reported that it received $18.6 million in gifts and grants from 23,438 donors. "Of this, $13,285,520 was in cash, qualifying the University for the first $6 million Ford Foundation grant," the *Notre Dame* development publication reported in spring 1964. "The unprecedented support included gifts averaging $345 from a record 80 percent of Notre Dame alumni. The funds are being used in overall University development, including construction of the 13-story Notre Dame Memorial Library, believed to be the largest library building in the world, which will be formally dedicated May 7."

A May 1964 article by Joe Lemon in the student news magazine the *Scholastic* offered an update on the Library's price tag. It said the cost of building the structure had totaled between $9.5 and $10 million, with additional infrastructure—such as drainage facilities needed to accommodate the building—raising the figure to about $12 million. In an earlier document from the University Archives titled *Problems in Planning Library Faciltiies,* Victor Schaefer is quoted in confirmation of that price tag: "Our President speaks of the building as costing $12 million, but I think he is adding to it all of the other costs involved with regard to preparing the site and redoing the power house. As I indicated, the building is air-conditioned throughout, and, as a result, this did mean extensive remodeling and increase of the power plant. We are going to have a central air-conditioning system on that side of the campus, which will also be used for all of the other new buildings to go up."

LOCATION, LOCATION, LOCATION

Father Ted elevated the Memorial Library from the status of vision to the status of a green-lighted project on December 1, 1959, when he made it the focus of an address to the Notre Dame faculty. Later that month, he gave a talk to Indianapolis-area alumni on the same subject, reports Marsha Stevenson in *What is Written Remains.* The university president announced that the library project he had been championing would move ahead, and he noted that a possible location would be the area of Cartier Field, the site where the Fighting Irish had first played, under the coaching of Knute Rockne, before Notre Dame Stadium was built just to the south. These remarks implied that discussions of the location for the new library were both important and incomplete.

Father Ted's clear belief that a new library would be central to the university's mission and identity went hand-in-hand with an initial notion that the building should literally be located at what was considered the center of the campus.

"Initial drawings placed the library—and a new administration building—at the site of Notre Dame's famed Main Building, at the core of the Notre Dame campus," writes Villanova University architectural historian Margaret Grubiak, in her comprehensive study, "Visualizing the Modern Catholic University: The Original Intention of 'Touchdown Jesus' at the University of Notre Dame." The idea made sense to a number of people for a number of reasons, Grubiak wrote in the journal, *Material Religion*, in 2010.

"The desire to elevate the reputation of Catholic higher education carried special importance for the location of the new library on the Notre Dame campus." A library standing at the head of Notre Dame Avenue and adjacent to the Church of the Sacred Heart (later made a basilica) "would visibly inaugurate a new era of academic achievement" while also sending a strong message of Catholic identity.

The existing Main Building, built in 1879, had lost some of its luster as a central showpiece because it badly needed extensive renovation. It lacked air conditioning and elevators, and its fifth floor had been closed off. Foregoing the expensive repairs in favor of a new complex with modern architecture would proclaim a "twentieth-century Notre Dame," as the *Scholastic* put it in a 1958 article by Jim Rose.

Another argument for that location was set forth by library director Victor Schaefer in a memo he submitted to Father Moore, academic assistant to the president, in May of 1959. "If there is one word which best describes an essential function of a library, it is 'accessibility,'" he wrote—noting that this meant not only keeping books and other resources physically close to patrons, but also making the building geographically convenient to members of the campus community. The Main Building location, Schaefer pointed out, had all of the university's residence halls and academic buildings within a 1,500-foot radius—something that could not be said for a building to the west, like the existing University Library, or a building to the east, where Cartier Field lay.

But at least one consideration trumped all these arguments—namely, the need to preserve Our Lady and her golden dome as a centerpiece of the campus. A desire to preserve this sacrosanct presence prompted many imaginative ideas and sketches, some envisioning the dome placed atop a more modern, modular structure, some seeing it as the cap of a tower or a column, standing as a monument in a courtyard, as Grubiak points out. But no plot to separate Our Lady from the Main Building proved architecturally acceptable. One might say that Our Lady on the dome helped to save the Main Building from the wrecking ball.

Grubiak, citing university documents, says the crucial decision came in June 1960: Build the library on the east side of campus, just north of Notre Dame Stadium, where this new edifice could add focus and architectural force to a part of campus that offered future expansion possibilities. The architectural firm of Ellerbe and Company, founded in 1909 and longtime partners with the university on various projects, was tasked with drawing up a plan for the library in this location.

Ellerbe and Company of St. Paul, Minnesota, headed since 1921 by architect Thomas Farr Ellerbe (son of the founder Franklin Ellerbe), already had a good relationship with Father Ted's executive vice president and close confidant, Rev. Edmund Joyce, C.S.C., known by the nickname of Father Ned. Ellerbe had already designed many of the campus's most notable post–World War II buildings, including O'Shaughnessy Hall of Liberal and Fine Arts, as well as the Art Gallery and the Keenan and Stanford residence halls.

Of course, this choice of the future location would require sacrificing some components of Notre Dame's past. The remnants of Cartier Field's athletic legacy—a baseball field, a track, and a football practice area—had to go, along with a Navy drill hall. That hall was immediately to the east of the Fieldhouse, where students assembled for football rallies and basketball games.

Also doomed was Vetville, the humble housing complex that had been cobbled together from war-surplus structures in 1946 for married World War II veterans. These veterans, and their growing families, swept onto the campus scene in the post-war years with financial help from the G.I. Bill. Even though this area was hardly at the campus's core, it occupied an important part of Father Ted's heart because he had been the chaplain for the many families who resided in Vetville during the late 1940s and early 1950s. But this was a new time—a time for a modern library. By 1961, replacement housing for married students would be under construction northwest of campus, to be dubbed the University Village complex.

Father Ted continued to see the library as part of a "trilogy"—along with the Basilica and the Golden Dome—connecting to the geographical and historical core of Notre Dame's identity. This third part of the trilogy would be about the future. Its arguably peripheral section of campus would be transformed as a center of modernity, reflecting a great Catholic university in the front ranks of modern higher education. As described in a 1960 booklet prepared to help fund-raising, "the library will be located on the East campus, near numerous post–World War II edifices including O'Shaughnessy Hall of Liberal and Fine Arts, the Nieuwland Science Center, Keenan and Stanford residence halls, the University's television and radio studios, and the North Dining Hall."

As plans for the new building developed, they merged into broader visions for the areas just north and south of the Library. To the north, there would eventually be space for students—without well-defined sketches as yet, but highly desirable for residence halls close enough to the academic core to keep Notre Dame a "walkable" campus. Already in the offing was a student activities center—the Stepan Center. It was built in 1962, likely one of the earlier geodesic dome facilities located on a college campus. To the south, the architects envisioned a quadrangle between the Library and the stadium—a sprawling place for buildings associated with science and research. A state-of-the-art radiation laboratory, funded by the U.S. Atomic Energy Commission, was planned as one of the Library's closest neighbors, as Grubiak reported in her *Material Religion* article. It was opened in 1964. A computing center was deemed a crucial neighbor for the Library, largely intended as a home for the giant Sperry Rand Universal Automatic Computer (Univac 1107) that the Library and other research buildings would utilize. Construction of this Information Technology Center exceeded the Library's construction pace and was completed in 1962.

This zone of progress extending from the Library was a captivating concept unto itself, without any reference to the stadium that would anchor the quad at its southern end. (University Architect Douglas Marsh points out that the anchor is actually a bit askew, a fact hardly perceptible to the naked eye: The stadium—and the Joyce Center which was built parallel to it—are "not perfectly on axis with the Library. . . . The stadium is actually skewed slightly to the northeast, which can only suggest that the surveyors misaligned it slightly." After all, there wasn't much nearby to align the new stadium with in 1930. "But the Library is parallel to everything else, in alignment with the rest of campus.")

Was the stadium's visual connection to "Touchdown Jesus" purely coincidental? Despite the stadium's prominence as part of the Notre Dame story, it is difficult to find any reference to that structure (or to football or touchdowns) in any of the materials promoting the Memorial Library or the quad it would help to create. Ironically, there was an indirect reference in the blessing that Joseph Cardinal Ritter prayed over the Library on May 7, 1964. He seemed to evoke a sports metaphor dismissing, rather than highlighting, the status of the stadium. His prayer honored the Library as "this majestic arena of the human spirit on the campus of the university dedicated to thy Immaculate Mother, Our Lady, Notre Dame du Lac."

Indifferent to any attention that might arise from future spectators in the stadium, architects still could claim three reasons to build the library facing south. The primary reason was anticipation of this zone of progress accentuating science and research—a new quad with the Library and the stadium serving as bookends. (Far from shunning or overshadowing the stadium, the construction of the Library and its pairing with the quad's southern bookend "brings the stadium into the campus," says University Architect Marsh.) A second consideration might have been the already busy zone on the Library's west wing, where the giant Fieldhouse dominated the connection to the campus's core. Third was consistency; the same southern-facing orientation was designed into such key buildings as the Basilica and the Main Building.

The resulting choice of a southern face had implications for the mural that would decorate the building's front tower wall. The face of Christ would soon be looking out upon the stadium, privileging generations of football fans with a remarkable view towering over the north goal posts. One might say figuratively that the view puts all the pieces of the Notre Dame mosaic—faith and reason, tradition and modernity, solemnity and fun—in especially high definition.

There is nothing peripheral about this eastern section of campus. While the stadium is a center of attention on many weekends during the year, the Library's location has made it a crossroads for day-to-day life on the campus. The concourse that grants entry into the building from south, east, and west, connecting the parking lots to the traditional campus core, continues to be traversed by thousands of people every day. The Library Quad has been the site of major gatherings for prayer, including not only the Dedication Mass in 1964 but a Mass for peace in 1969 and a Mass marking the tenth anniversary of the September 11, 2001, terrorist attacks.

BUILDING ON THE DREAM

With limited attention to the football field just down the path, Notre Dame started building a Memorial Library that would cover roughly the acreage of nearly two football fields. The structure itself would contain almost 430,000 square feet of space on thirteen floors, making credible its claim to be the largest college library in the country at the time.

Everybody had an idea about how to build the Library. One key influence at the time was the notion that a university library should be, in a sense, two libraries—one for the undergraduates and one for the graduate students. "Many institutions across the United States felt a need to develop a core academic collection that would support the undergraduate learning experience as distinct from the specialized research collection available in the rest of the library," explains James Neal, Columbia University's vice president for information services and former assistant director and advisory council member for the Hesburgh Libraries.

It wasn't just books that people needed. Technology was advancing. Microfilm was a growing phenomenon. Much information was contained in audiovisual form, from radio to stereo recordings to film and beyond. "If the impact of television is not immediately obvious, some day it will be," library director Schaefer wrote in one of his planning memos, "and provision must be made not only for closed circuit television but also for kinescopes, video tape, and other visual instructional facilities."

The Library was always conceived as still more than a place for books and gadgets. It was to be a place for people, including undergraduate and graduate students as well as faculty and staff. The goal was to have a comfortable setting where nearly half of the student body could be seated at one time. "Seating" meant a diversity of productive study space—group study rooms, closed carrels, open carrels with peripheral privacy, typing rooms, and basic tables and chairs. There were even smoking lounges.

Whenever possible, in keeping with modern library design, the people were to be seated in close proximity to the books they were accessing, as described in the *Notre Dame* development publication. This led to a plan for specialization of space—dedicating the first floor to the humanities, with areas further broken down into groupings like philosophy/theology, art/music, and language/literature. As described in archived documents, the second floor was planned to house social studies, with separate areas for European history, American history, the social sciences, business, and general science. The most advanced works on physics and other sciences would remain where they had been shelved elsewhere on campus, but the plan was to give the Memorial Library a core collection representing science for the well-educated layperson.

A library for people, not just books, had special implications for Notre Dame faculty. They too were a growing population on campus. They would be provided not only with seating, but with office space. The library's lower level, the basement, was designed to hold offices for up to 248 faculty members, though reports differ on the exact number of offices that eventually were occupied. This location afforded these scholars the ultimate proximity to the ultimate collection of resources in thirteen stories above them. The basement would have a separate entrance that faculty members could use at any time, day or night.

The Library was planned to be the center for other aspects of academic life, supporting numerous faculty and staff. Designs allowed the tower to contain headquarters for various scholarly pursuits, including the Medieval Institute and the Jacques Maritain Center, as well as the University Archives.

Incorporating all of these ideas, Ellerbe and Company imposed a certain simplicity and modularity in the building's design, heeding the modernist architectural maxim, "form follows function." As architectural historian Margaret Grubiak points out, Ellerbe served up a building very clearly designed in two parts—an eleven-story tower designed as a "Research Library," rising from a sprawling, two-story, U-shaped base designed as a "College Library," where the university's undergraduates could gather, interact, and study. This library would hold about 200,000 of the projected two million books.

The tower housed additional resources ideal for faculty members and graduate students— seminar rooms, specialized libraries, offices for centers and institutes, enclosed study carrels, and

43

44

an endless space for books—that remained accessible to undergraduates. The base held a wide selection of books with complete open-stack access, plus an Audio Learning Center, microfilm reading space, and plentiful study areas.

Interior decoration of the building was planned with an eye to comfort and an inviting sense of luxury, Grubiak reported. The materials used—marble, walnut, oak paneling—worked together with the furnishings, textures, and colors to make a hospitable place for study. The vastness of the first two floors—purposely maximizing the modular flexibility that planners wanted—could also be masked by creating "people pockets" with furniture amid the rows of stacks. A thirty-year veteran of the Notre Dame faculty recalls that most of the open areas on the second

floor wound up reflecting hospitality more than study, as they became centers for undergraduate get-togethers. Students inclined toward more earnest studying retreated to private study rooms and quieter corners of the tower floors.

The first floor, comprising 76,000 square feet, was designed to hold library musts like the circulation desk and card catalog. It welcomed visitors into this central area from three directions—from the south, where people entered through the main entrance, and from the east and west thanks to the long concourse stretching from parking lots to the Fieldhouse. Those traversing this campus intersection would pass such concourse attractions as an auditorium, a faculty lounge, the space for special collections, and tributes to benefactors who had made the library possible. (The faculty lounge, until its transformation into a vending area and most recently into an "Au Bon Pain" restaurant, was a quiet place with a carpeted floor and comfortable armchairs, couches, and coffee tables. Faculty members occasionally used the space for small meetings and receptions.)

The second floor was larger than the first, with 92,000 square feet. This created an overhang surmounting the first floor—a cornice around the building, supported by pillars (also called pilotis) rising from the ground. The first story exterior was to be covered in polished tweed granite. The second story exterior was covered in the distinctive multicolored face brick supplied by the Belden Brick Company of Canton, Ohio. Grubiak calls this a "nod to context" since so many other buildings on campus have the Belden Brick look. Indeed, the standards for design and construction published by the Office of the University Architect in 2008 still specified that face brick for new construction is to be provided by Belden unless otherwise approved.

Rising from the two-story base would be an eleven-story tower—actually a twelve-story structure, counting the penthouse, which would contain meeting areas and would offer grand views of the campus (notably including the other two parts of Father Ted's "trilogy" and the stadium). Beneath the penthouse, the tower was to be covered with buff-colored Mankato stone, a variety of limestone containing more than 49 percent calcium carbonate, with about 4.5 percent alumina and some silica.

The tower would have at least two numerical features likely to prompt remarks by particularly attentive passengers in the building's four primary elevators. Visitors would notice there is indeed a button for the thirteenth floor—despite the fact that many buildings across the country, at least in their signage, leapfrog from twelve to fourteen for reasons of superstition. However, three of the Library's elevators have no button for the third floor. This floor was designed as a non-visitor level given over to mechanical equipment. In addition, transport to the fourteenth floor penthouse is restricted, with elevator buttons for that floor requiring key access.

One design factor that contributed to the Library's distinctive appearance was the matter of windows. Library designers of the period disagreed about the use of windows. Some argued against windows, saying a stack area needs constant, reliable lighting conditions, without the sun's glare, along with good temperature control, as Stevenson points out. What's more, a broad vista outside only serves as a distraction from studies anyway. This viewpoint won out with Ellerbe, at least in the design of the tower. Father Ted himself has said that the scarcity of windows risked making the Library look like a grain storage silo—one key reason to place a mural on the tower wall. On the first floor, however, most notably in the area that for years served as the periodicals reading room, the design called for lots of windows all around, and the second floor, too, lets the sun shine in, upon student tables and staff work areas alike. (In more recent times, the whole debate about windows in libraries has largely disappeared, helped by the development of glass treatments blocking out the ultraviolet rays that can damage books.)

The Library's design came under attack early and often for not fitting in with the rest of the campus. But the fact is that the building was meant to be big and distinctive—to send an unmistakable message "about the importance attached to scholarly achievement by the institution," as Stevenson writes. She quotes library director Victor Schaefer explaining the design during a 1963 Library Buildings Institute symposium: "There was a very simple factor that influenced what kind of a building we would have. . . . The President [Father Ted] wanted to have a building which would be the dominant building on the campus, and I think we have that."

A representative from Ellerbe also was eloquent when he was asked to explain the Library's design in apparent opposition to the rest of the tradition-rich campus. He wrote in a 1960 letter, as quoted by Stevenson, "One cannot really relate this as a known historical style, but rather allows it to conform with the traditional functional buildings prevailing on campus today, therefore the building belongs. Perhaps this is its style: to belong in harmony with the total campus—past, present, and future!"

The notion of allowing the building to conform, and to belong, in the broadest context of the university, including both its traditions and its future, was on target and prescient. The Library was indeed a testament to both and has come to fit in as a beloved icon of Notre Dame fifty years later.

REAL AND ENDURING

As a practical matter, the "future" began for the Memorial Library with the groundbreaking after commencement in 1961, followed by a formal blessing of the site in August, according to the *South Bend Tribune*. The construction was under way.

In April of 1962, Father Ted literally made his mark on the building. Before the highest structural beam was hoisted into place, he inscribed onto it a Latin phrase: "*Nos cum prole pia benedicat Virgo Maria*"—a time-honored Catholic prayer that Father Ted translates, "May the Blessed Mother bless us with her wonderful child."

During the months that followed, students were known to occasionally enter the off-limits construction site and climb high into the skyscraper's skeleton. In May of 1963 as reported in the *South Bend Tribune,* a student tragically fell 168 feet to his death from the top of the thirteenth floor.

August of 1963 brought the big transfer of books for which library director Schaefer had spent more than a year planning. According to the *Scholastic,* some 475,000 books from the University Library were packed in 2,000 beer cartons and moved to the new building by conveyor belts and other means. Not only was the departure from the old building complicated, but the totally new layout and organizational scheme in the new building—with specialized mini-departments on the first two floors, for example—also required intricate logistics, as pointed out by reporter Roger Birdsell in the *South Bend Tribune* at the time.

The Library opened in September of 1963 so that students could start the fall semester with access to books, but there was more work to be done. *The Word of Life* mural was attached to the front wall of the tower during the spring of 1964, clearing the way for the aforementioned dedication ceremonies in May.

Father Ted's prayer to Mary written onto the steelwork is a reminder that the Library was destined to be prominent but not entirely dominant as a presence on campus. At about 210 feet tall, it is said to be nearly equal in height to the statue of Our Lady on the dome. Both are shorter than the top of the cross on the spire of the Basilica of the Sacred Heart, at 218 feet. (That remains the maximum height for campus buildings today, says University Architect Doug Marsh.) The Library is therefore the most modern, but not the most monumental, of Father Ted's "trilogy" of buildings.

The new Library allowed the 1917 University Library to be reborn as the home of the Notre Dame School of Architecture. After the departure of the books, the architecture school's highly regarded leader Frank Montana spearheaded the building's modification in the 1960s. A more substantial makeover would wait until the 1990s, when the building was renamed Bond Hall, in gratitude to a benefactor whose gift allowed substantial reconstruction.

In many ways, the University Library of 1917 vintage and the Memorial Library of 1964 vintage could not be more different. But Notre Dame's gift for patterns that connect past and future can be seen even in a comparison of these two buildings. Note four similarities.

The Memorial Library's location was selected largely to create a new quadrangle suited to the university's growth plans. As Stevenson points out, the University Library's site was selected more than forty years earlier to initiate a new quad, too—close to the Main Building but composed primarily of dormitories.

The Memorial Library's modernism was clearly a sharp break from the University's customary architectural style. But in its own time, the 1917 University Library, or Lemonnier Library, with its distinctive classical style, was likewise unique. Now, as Bond Hall, "it is a wonderful building and aptly serves as the home for the School of Architecture," says Domer architect Marsh, who adds: "Like thousands of 'Arkies' since 1962, I spent a lot of my college life in that building."

As testified in so much of the anticipatory literature about the Memorial Library, and indeed as reaffirmed in the ceremonies surrounding its construction and dedication, the building symbolized an assertion of hope at a time of great change and tension. John Fitzgerald Kennedy had become the first Catholic to serve as president of the United States, and the spirit of Camelot was in the air, but an assassin struck down JFK about two months after the Library opened. The Cold War was in full swing, and conflicts both at home and abroad were poised to grow. The University Library's dedication in June 1917 came less than two months after the United States' entry into the tumult of World War I. But there were also glimmers of hope in that year, at least two of them pertinent to Notre Dame: Knute Rockne was named head coach of the Fighting Irish football team after the 1917 season, and Theodore Martin Hesburgh was born in Syracuse, New York.

Designing Wisdom

The Memorial Library's design to house two million volumes represented an ambitious leap from the 500,000 books that the university held at the time. Stevenson reveals that the University Library was planned to house nearly 618,000 volumes, representing a remarkable vision of growth in light of the fact that the University's 1917 collection contained only about 100,000 books. Dreaming big, welcoming change, and confronting anxious times with zeal and optimism are clearly nothing new for Notre Dame.

Chapter Two

FIDES ET LECTIO

Now that the building was complete, perhaps it did look a bit like a grain silo or grain elevator, as Father Ted had cautioned. Indeed, some students were said to have dubbed it the "brain silo."

THE MAN WHO GOT THE PICTURE

But Father Ted had an answer to that in his mind even before the building went up. In his travels around the world, he had seen countless university libraries. Among those was the Central Library at the Universidad Nacional Autónoma de México (UNAM) in Mexico City. That library, too, is a largely windowless tower standing upon a base. But it is certainly not visually dull.

Colorful mosaic murals, completed in 1953, cover all four sides of the UNAM tower. Father Ted was especially struck by one mural that featured huge Aztec iconography, juxtaposed with symbols of Hispanic and Catholic colonization but ultimately representing a victory for Mexican nationalism and modernization. As architectural historian Margaret Grubiak puts it, the library image suggested "an inimical relationship between Catholicism and academic inquiry."

The imagery flowed from UNAM's identity as a public university, intentionally symbolizing a rejection of control by the Catholic Church so as to emphasize its academic freedom. Father Ted wanted to respond that, to the contrary, Catholic identity was profoundly

compatible with academic freedom in the search for truth, and he wanted to make this point with an equally powerful, towering image.

Thus, it was no surprise that even the early drawings of a proposed Memorial Library included a mural on its façade. Furthermore, the concept of Christ the Teacher—not an enemy to knowledge but indeed the focal point of all truth for his followers through the ages—became a guiding theme. Howard and Evangeline Phalin stepped forward as benefactors willing to support the $200,000 cost of the mural project. Howard, a member of the Notre Dame class of 1928 and member of the University's Board of Trustees, had married his wife in the Log Chapel. As reported in the Library's *Access* newsletter, he had a lifelong love of books and retired in 1968 as chairman of the board of the Field Enterprises Educational Corporation, publisher of the *World Book* encyclopedia. (The mural's price tag is reported, among other places, in *What is Written Remains.*)

With the basic concept and funding in place, it was time to find an artist to create the mural. Ellerbe and Company approached Millard Sheets, a nationally known California artist born in 1907 who had built a reputation working as a painter, watercolorist, muralist, architectural designer, art professor, writer, and overall multimedia prodigy. By 1930, his work had been selected to be part of Carnegie Institute's International Exhibition of Art, one of the most respected such exhibitions in the country. Reflecting the artist's popular appeal, a number of bank branch buildings throughout California were designed and decorated by him, presenting beautiful landscapes of nature and scenes of community. According to the university publication, *The Word of Life,* Sheets had even served as a war correspondent, covering events of World War II in art and words for *Life* magazine.

Ellerbe had worked with Sheets when he designed a mural for a Mayo Clinic diagnostic center in Minnesota in 1953, according to the biography *Millard Sheets: One-Man Renaissance,* by Janice Lovoos and Edmund F. Penney. His fame had continued to grow since then. In 1962, after

56

winning a national design competition, he had been commissioned to create a 60-by-22-foot mural for the exterior of the Detroit Public Library.

This Detroit library project was, in a sense, the start of something big. "Sheets selected as an organizational motif the concept that ideas flow like a river and libraries house the best of these ideas," the biographers said of the Detroit design. "He used very large symbolic figures in the center and on two sides, with smaller figures in the center and on two sides, with smaller figures tying them all together. Interesting detail was included; as a result the finished piece reads well both from a distance and up close. This is not always the case with large murals, because when the scale doubles, for example, from six to twelve feet, problems of proportion also multiply rather than diminish. To achieve simplicity and power in the forms required concentration and care."

With these and many other artistic triumphs to recommend Sheets, the Ellerbe architectural firm submitted his name to Notre Dame officials, along with a dozen other potential artists, according to *One-Man Renaissance*. The firm knew that the mural being considered at Notre Dame, at 134 feet high by 68 feet wide, was much more than double the Detroit mural's size.

Father Ted, in a 2003 speech recalling the Memorial Library project at a dedication event for the Library's renovated lower level, said he was pleased with the feedback he had received from Sheets when he told him his ideas for a mural—ideas drawn partly from the UNAM library mural in Mexico. Questioned more recently for this book, Father Ted said there was no serious consideration given to other artists or visual concepts.

"It didn't take much encouragement to inspire Millard to share the vision," Father Ted said. "Artists are people of vision, and Millard was a wonderful artist in many media. . . . I shared my concept with him knowing that we needed something spectacular to take this enormous building in the middle of a prairie in northern Indiana and not have it look like a grain elevator."

Sheets, who likewise would have had no reason to be thinking of clever connections with football, embraced the idea of Christ as master teacher, and he let it drive his artistic genius in many exciting directions for design and execution.

In a 1964 interview with Father Jerome Wilson, C.S.C., Notre Dame's vice president for business affairs and overseer of the campus's physical plant, Sheets said "the wonderful sense of

Fides et Lectio

freedom that the University of Notre Dame gave me was, first of all, a real challenge: How can you give some sense of the rich depository of ideas that man has contributed over the centuries?"

In a separate 1964 interview with *Scholastic* magazine, he explained how his creativity proceeded: "The theme, of course, was suggested by the Notre Dame administration. What they asked me to do was to suggest in a great processional the idea of a never-ending line of great scholars, thinkers, and teachers—saints that represented the best that man has recorded, and which are found represented in a library. The thought was that the various periods that are suggested in the theme have unfolded in the continuous process of one generation giving to the next. I put Christ at the top with the disciples to suggest that He is the great teacher—that is really the thematic idea."

Sheets explained that he started with the giant cross as a uniting element, tying together the mural from side to side and top to bottom. The cross's light color was common ground uniting the mural with the light stone background chosen by Ellerbe for the tower.

FROM CONTEMPLATION TO CONSTRUCTION

Art and architecture also had to find common ground in terms of the material to be used for the mural. "The engineers were adamant that granite was the only feasible material for a mosaic mural," according to Lovoos and Penney. "The extremes of heat and cold that mark the climate in South Bend dictated this material, stressed one particularly vehement man. This opinion influenced Sheets, and he investigated potential colors and textures with which he could expect to design the mural. He put to work friends and stone brokers around the world, searching out unusual tones of granite; eventually the tally of colors reached an amazing 143 shades."

Sheets, in consultation with his Notre Dame partners, particularly Father Ted and Father Ned, doggedly pursued both design and implementation. After a year of preliminary work, a complete, detailed design for the mural was made, and granite colors—from white to black with many grays and varied tints of red, pink, green, and blue and gold—were selected. Sheets laid out the mural, in a format called a cartoon. The pattern was divided into a grid with squares measuring 10 feet by 10 feet.

Of course, the design and plan for implementation needed official approval from Notre Dame. The Reverend Carolyn Sheets Owen-Towle, Millard's daughter and a retired Unitarian Universalist minister, recounted the adventurous story of that approval process when she gave a speech at the same 2003 event where Father Ted recalled his early meeting with the artist. "The cartoon had to be brought here to South Bend to be inspected and approved by Father Joyce, who was overseeing the project," she said. "When artist and cartoon arrived, it was clear that there was no indoor space large enough to place it from which it could fully be viewed. . . . As they scratched their heads, Father Joyce suggested the water tower here on campus next to which, at that time, spread an open field. The cartoon was carefully laid out on the field with all the sections coming together to form the whole. Then, the artist and Father Joyce proceeded to climb the water tower."

Lovoos and Penney tell the story of the ninety-foot climb in more detail:

It was a Midwestern winter day, and a strong wind was blowing. Sheets thought the climb would not be too difficult, though, since the ladder that snaked up the side had a slight tilt and railings; he neglected to note that the last section of the climb would be up a narrow

61

vertical arrangement of rungs and that the top of the water tower was not flat but, rather, slightly pointed. Father Joyce . . . insisted on accompanying Sheets up the tower. Sheets demurred, pointing out to the priest that his elegant robe and tricornered hat would be severely damaged by such an exertion. Joyce insisted, and after removing his hat, followed Sheets up the side of the tower.

Resolutely the two men climbed higher and higher. After ascending the final icy rung, they found that they still could not see the ground because of the tower's inclined top. So, very gingerly, they slid down on their stomachs toward the tower's edge. There, they saw that all the risk was worthwhile: the mural's values and lines carried beautifully.

The Reverend Owen-Towle added a personal recollection during her 2003 speech, recalling how her father made the tower story part of the family's oral tradition for her and the other Sheets children. "Dad loved telling us, as we'd clutch our stomachs, that the climb up the tower was not the particularly difficult part, nor even bellying up the slope of the tower's top, although that was edgy," Owen-Towle recalled. "But, bellying down the downward slope to get a view—that was terrifying. I've always imagined that this must have been the world's most instantly approved project of art."

Regardless of its speed, approval was only the beginning of a very complex process of executing the plan. After final checks of the granite colors and textures and shapes were made, master stone craftsmen at what Jack Rowe of *Scholastic* magazine called the world's largest granite works, the Cold Spring Granite Company in Cold Spring, Minnesota, started cutting the stone. They reportedly accomplished an unprecedented feat—cutting granite on a curve. The granite itself came in from various parts of the United States as well as Europe, Africa, South America, and Australia. According to Notre Dame geologist Erhard Winkler, 81 different stones, in 171 finishes, from 16 countries, were used. Other materials, such as limestone and gneiss, were also in the mix. *American Artist* magazine reported that the approximately 6,000 pieces of granite ranged in size from about three inches square to six feet by nine feet and also varied sharply in thickness. (Documents found in the University Archives contain some discrepancies about the details of the mural. For example, Winkler said, in a magazine piece in the 1960s, the dimensions of the mural were 132 feet high by 65 feet wide, not the 134 feet by 68 feet measurement found [along with other heights and widths] in other University records. Notre Dame's own booklet, *The Word of Life,* quotes Sheets's daughter, Rev. Carolyn Sheets Owen-Towle as saying there are 7,000 pieces of granite, up to a thousand above quantities cited by some others.)

John W. Stamper, associate dean of the School of Architecture, explains in a Notre Dame video, *The Word of Life,* how the pieces were assembled: Stainless steel dowels were attached, and

workers putting the mural in place "coated all of it with plastic before covering it with cement. When it was then installed on the building, there was actually a space between the structural elements of the building and the mural itself, so the whole thing can expand and contract and move very slightly during the changing seasons."

The process of actually attaching 324 panels containing all the pieces to the Library's tower wall took place during the spring semester of 1964, with completion in time for the May dedication. The assembly efforts, mostly accomplished behind the cover of a curtain, yielded an attention-grabbing result—a colossal piece of art that may still be among the largest granite mural-mosaics in the world.

The 1964 *American Artist* story about Sheets and his masterpiece doesn't honor this accomplishment with top ranking in any particular artistic category. Instead, it points out the challenge of categorizing the mural at all. The author, Frederic Whitaker, assessed the end-result this way: "It cannot be called a mosaic, for the parts are so enormous; nor can those parts be called tesserae, for the same reason. They are measured in feet and yards rather than by inches. [Tesserae are the small bits of glass and stone typically associated with a mosaic.] Perhaps *intarsia* would come nearest to a definition of the method." However, intarsia has typically involved the setting of stones other than granite into marble, so even that term is problematic.

WHAT'S IN A NAME?

Regardless of how one defines this mural, it is easy to call it unique. It literally leaves a huge impression, and it has continued to capture imaginations for fifty years.

Christ is the dominant figure in a story that transcends and unites the ages. The mural uses Christ the Teacher, the Word of Life, as a unifying component and boldly proclaims Him as central to the university. Christ's presence gives dimension to the background cross as a unifying image. The cross, a symbol of death, becomes the indispensable context for resurrection, as well as a procession of witnesses, recalling the Congregation of Holy Cross watchword, "Hail the Cross, our only Hope."

Sheets noted in a 1964 interview that he had taken pains to add touches of enduring interest and ongoing surprise into the mural: no one should be bored by seeing *The Word of Life* multiple times, he said. Sheets had added diagonal lines, representing rays of light, as a key element of the image, breaking it up in cubist fashion, shedding light on the characters but also placing some in differing degrees of shadow. He commented that the lines inject "a kind of mystery and excitement" in the mural. The different shapes, colors, and textures of the granite guaranteed that the mural would change subtly as time passed during the day.

The artist and all those involved in the building also wanted the mural to be enduring, as enduring as truth itself. First and foremost, the mural should be understood.

Sheets provided a diagram that explained the mural. It can be found on a plaque near the south end of the Library's neighboring reflecting pool, which itself serves as an amplifier for the art's beauty and message. The key to the diagram outlines the sections of the mural and shows how the story of the mural not only proceeds from the top down—with Christ as the teacher calling all unto himself from on high—but also from the bottom up. No fewer than fifty devotees of wisdom rise chronologically in procession, from ancient classic cultures near the base of the mural to "Prophets of the Old Testament," followed by "Christians of the Early Church," and various historical periods, culminating in the "Age of Science and Exploration."

Another panel of the explanatory plaque by the reflecting pool presents an inspiring description of the figures in the procession, the meaning of the mural, and the connection between mural and Library:

> From the symbol of all Christianity, the cross, emerges the figure of Christ, the greatest of teachers. He, the Word of Life. The only begotten of the Father was from the beginning,

with Father and Holy Spirit, in eternal divine life. Became man of the Blessed Virgin, He was seen and looked upon by human eyes and His voice was heard upon the earth. Loving ears listed to His words, and minds were inspired to remember and to note them down, and the ineffable New Testament took shape: the deeds and words of Christ, the primary document of Christian wisdom, the word of life, and of life-giving truth.

With Him in spirit are gathered the saints, the scholars, the scribes, and the teachers stretching through time, who have dedicated themselves to the preservation of truth, the Word of Life, and the preparation of men's minds to receive that truth. Their knowledge, their thoughts, their written word, which through the ages have illuminated and enriched the understanding of their own and succeeding generations, is the treasure house of knowledge housed within the walls of this structure.

The natural richness and subtlety of the stone, as well as its permanence, make it a fitting material to emphasize the grandeur, complexity, and timelessness of man's search for the truth. The truth, which is serenely and eternally possessed in the divine Person of the Word.

This profound summation was written by Father Ted and Rev. Charles E. Sheedy, C.S.C., who was a theology professor and dean of the College of Arts and Letters at the time of the mural's debut. Father Ted explained in a 2003 speech that he had asked his good friend, Father Sheedy, to write "a little essay." He continued, "I think that's a beautiful little piece of prose as well, that, in an unusual way, catches the spirit of Millard's inspiration." This weather-worn, often ignored, plaque by the reflecting pool may be the definitive—and perhaps the original—declaration of the mural's title.

Notably, the generations of truth-seekers pictured in the mural are not disclosed as specific individuals (although one crowned figure is purported to be King David with his lyre in the section devoted to the Hebrew Scriptures). Rather, these disciples of the Teacher are presented in groups; they are important as members of a community and followers in procession, pursuing knowledge in order to share it and pass it along.

Endurance was key to the mural in another way, too. Physical durability, given South Bend's harsh winters and temperature variability, was a major reason for the use of granite and other design elements. Interestingly, the setting of the mural, facing south toward Notre Dame Stadium, contributed to the durability. Father Wilson, in his interview with Sheets, commented that a geologist on Notre Dame's faculty had called the southern wall a fortunate choice to be the palette upon which the artist worked.

Sheets agreed with this analysis. Granite is very dense, he said, but "it still does have a small percentage of water absorption. So being on the south [there] will never be any serious damage

to the surface of the material because whatever moisture might be absorbed for a moment will be immediately dried out with the sun."

Just as an array of elements and endeavors came together in the mural to make Sheets's two years of work an artistic triumph, many things about the mural—including its design and location, its powerful messages and inherent drama—came together to make it enduring and endearing, truly iconic, in the hearts of the Notre Dame community.

The name, *The Word of Life,* was one aspect of the mural that did not stick in many students' minds. Many called it "Christ the Teacher," according to one longtime faculty member. Other students greeted the mural with barbed wit; among its nicknames, according to Thomas Schlereth's *The University of Notre Dame: A Portrait of its History and Campus,* was "the world's largest holy card."

But the nickname that has had its own enduring prominence over the years is "Touchdown Jesus." Father Ted himself has said that, despite his lack of interest in football connections for the building and its mural, he considers the nickname a sign of affection—"a nice, friendly, familiar name for this beautiful piece of art."

It is difficult to say when and how the "Touchdown Jesus" moniker first came into use. The *Washington Post* sports section mentioned the nickname in a November 3, 1969, sports story, "Navy Given Lesson at Football U." The writer spends less time on Notre Dame's 47–0 romp over Navy than he does on Notre Dame's "shrine"-like aspects. He includes this passage in his verbal tour: "Notre Dame's new library has a mural of Christ the Teacher with arms upraised, facing directly over one of the goal posts. Not surprisingly, it is called 'Touchdown Jesus.'"

Noted sociologist Rev. Andrew Greeley mentions the term in his 1969 book, *From Backwater to Mainstream: A Profile of Catholic Higher Education.* One of his findings from the Notre Dame campus is this: "Some of the more irreverent students have nicknamed this mosaic 'Touchdown Jesus.'"

The mural's nickname has been borrowed for the titles of at least one novella and two non-fiction books. One of the books, *Touchdown Jesus: The Mixing of Sacred and Secular in American History,* is a 2003 study of how religion is interwoven into American popular culture. The other, *Touchdown Jesus: Faith and Fandom at Notre Dame,* is a sports reporter's 2005 tale of Fighting Irish intrigue. The author, Scott Eden, says this of the mural's name: "The precise etymology has been lost, but almost immediately after its unveiling in 1964, some campus wit or other created the nickname by which it is now colloquially and universally known. He or she should have taken out a copyright. Almost nobody knows its real title."

Eden may be right that somebody came up with the nickname shortly after the unveiling. *South Bend Tribune* sports editor emeritus Joe Doyle, a 1949 Notre Dame graduate who covered Fighting Irish football for decades, said in a 2012 interview that he recalled using "Touchdown

Jesus" in stories not long after the mural went up, and he probably had learned it from students. But others suggest the term was not likely to have spread quickly, at least in the national conversation about Notre Dame, because at the time such a witticism might have struck some Catholic hearts as too irreverent (to use Greeley's word) for public consumption. No published proof of that nickname showed up when in 2012 University Archivist Peter Lysy performed a search of the newly digitized archives of the *Scholastic* student magazine and *The Dome*, the student yearbook. No such name appeared in the 1964–1967 period. Another publication found in the University Archives, a freshman orientation booklet produced for students entering Notre Dame in the summer of 1968, made no mention of the mural nickname—although it seized an opportunity to be humorous. The booklet described the library only as "that tall building that looks like a drive-in movie with *Ben Hur* playing."

A reference to "Touchdown Jesus" was discovered in *Scholastic* magazine's October 4, 1968, issue, in a light-hearted section called "On Other Campuses." It quoted a "letter" from a member of the University of Oklahoma football team—a letter that reportedly had appeared in their campus newspaper after Notre Dame vanquished them 45–21 a few weeks earlier. The letter-writer, "Rocky," told his friend, "You are probably more interested in knowing why we lost the big game Saturday. . . . What I think is that we were out-religioned. I don't mean to sound sacrilegious or nothing, but it's the truth. I mean, how are you going to beat a team that is practically playing on their own church lawn? On one end of the stadium, the north end I think, there is a big library building, and on its side is a huge picture of Jesus. And, Al, I swear that he has his hands raised over his head as if he were signaling a touchdown. The people up there call him Touchdown

Fides et Lectio

Jesus. You can imagine what kind of effect that has on a team. I mean, you look up there and you see this huge painting looming over the stadium staring at you. How are you going to beat a team like that?" This Oklahoma letter-writer, whether real or fictional, captures the visceral nature of reactions to the mural.

The mural certainly became a visceral experience for Millard Sheets—something to be taken not lightly, but lovingly. For one thing, it consumed the greater part of two years of his life. As someone who embraced large-scale designs with powerful messages, integrating art and architecture, surprising and delighting people with an array of colors and techniques, Sheets had been given an ideal challenge. "This mosaic is an incredibly complicated and ambitious work that once again stretched him mightily and again rewarded his confidence," recalled his daughter Rev. Owen-Towle in her 2003 speech. "If Millard could conceive of something, it did not occur to him that he could not bring it off." That was seen, for example, in his rejection of the conventional wisdom that granite could not be cut on the curve. To give credit where it is due, it took the craftspeople of Cold Spring Granite Company to prove Sheets's confidence well-founded.

Sheets did indeed immerse himself in the project, conducting research about different kinds of granites—their colors, textures, and availability—from around the world, as mentioned above. In addition, "He definitely did Catholic history research," Owen-Towle recalled in a 2011 interview for this book. While not trying to identify fifty specific figures around Christ, he did give each group its own historically representative garb.

His deep love for art and for its impact on life made him willing to go to great lengths, just as the water tower incident made him go to great heights. His diligence about the Library reflected his belief that art could help a community appreciate its own inherent beauty and value. "Every time he built a building, he researched the history of the area so he knew what important history was there," his daughter recalled.

"He was neither a Catholic nor institutionally religious, but he was deeply evolved spiritu-ally," Owen-Towle added, noting her father's passion for bringing beauty to the world through art and helping others to see that beauty. Sheets understood the psychology of color and space, and he understood how to make someone's spirit soar, she said. She wrote this in *Damngorgeous,* her memoir of Sheets:"He was driven by some divine spark, impelled by a vision that he was on earth to increase the loveliness he found here. He painted to pass on the angels circulating in his wonder-filled mind, and he invited the rest of us to draw near, to open our eyes, to become co-celebrants alongside him."

Owen-Towle's own feelings about the mural are visceral and enduring, she acknowledged in her 2011 interview. "It's just awe-inspiring. I love the fact that the university had the imagination to create something so wonderful, and a lot of that goes to Father Hesburgh." She thanked Hes-burgh for the fact that "he made it possible for my father to do something like that."

She was sure that Sheets would not mind the playful term "Touchdown Jesus" being applied to the mural. She recalled Charles R. Loving, director of the Snite Museum of Art, when he commented in 2003 that this work of public art is iconic in the same sense as the Statue of Liberty. He had added that the mural has been granted *two* iconic meanings—"the Catholic Christian history and the great tradition of football here at the University of Notre Dame." She recalled the 2003 comments of Dennis Doordan, chair of the Department of Art, Art History, and Design, who said it's rare for a work of art to be "genuinely loved" and that the "Touchdown Jesus" nickname is a mark of that love.

In their 1964 interview, Sheets and Father Wilson sensed and discussed the love that had been expressed in and through the Memorial Library. They agreed that the workers who had helped to assemble both the building and the mural deserved a great deal of credit. "I have never seen such devotion" as he witnessed in the tireless, detailed work on thousands of pieces of stone at the Cold Spring Granite Company, Sheets said. He mused that the effort of those assembling the mural "is slightly like the devotion and dedication that must have existed at the time they built the great Gothic cathedrals." Father Wilson chimed in about the energy surrounding the project, saying "maybe there is something about this particular building" that excited everyone involved; "the steelworkers were the same way," he recalled.

Sheets went even further about the remarkable nature of the project. "I think this whole thing has been done on faith. I particularly enjoyed meeting the donor [Phalin] a few minutes ago. And talk about faith—this man had about as much faith as anybody could have had, to not have seen and experienced the step by step and blow by blow difficulty at times that we had, of course, in working this out. It has been a marvelous thing, and of course your faith here at Notre Dame has been one of the challenges of my life. I have enjoyed the job not because it is the biggest job, but because of the spirit of real collaboration and excitement about what it was we were trying to achieve."

There was yet another way in which the love that attached itself to the phenomenon of "Touchdown Jesus" was visceral for Millard Sheets. As his daughter put it, "In the process of creating and executing this work, Millard and [his wife] Mary became dear friends with Father Ted and Father Ned. Their friendship endured until my father's death in 1989."

If the faith of Notre Dame represented a challenge in this outstanding artist's life, he embraced it, at least partially, through his friendship with the priests. Moreover, one might say the faith embraced him. Among other religious masterpieces, Sheets went on to do more work for the Catholic Church, including the 3,340-square-foot mosaic, *Triumph of the Lamb,* which decorates the dome high above the sanctuary of the National Basilica of the Immaculate Conception in Washington, D.C.

SURROUNDED BY SPIRIT

Remarkably, the numerous reflections on hope and love that can be drawn from the *Word of Life* mural are only part of the spiritual impact that was designed into the Memorial Library. As architectural historian Margaret Grubiak has written, "The mural articulated for the University of Notre Dame a mission statement for the modern Catholic university, sanctioning academic freedom with the awareness and belief that Christ is its center and ultimate aim."

Right from the start, Ellerbe and Company spoke of an "art program," coordinated by art director Warren Towle Mosman, for the whole library project. Through that organized plan, a number of elements would come together to reaffirm the mission statement, and the university's expression of that mission, resoundingly around the building.

All around the first-floor perimeter of the Library, visitors are drawn into a walking tour that expands upon the mural towering above them. As part of the "art program," Ellerbe presented a procession of twenty images, engraved into the exterior granite walls. These etchings, inlaid

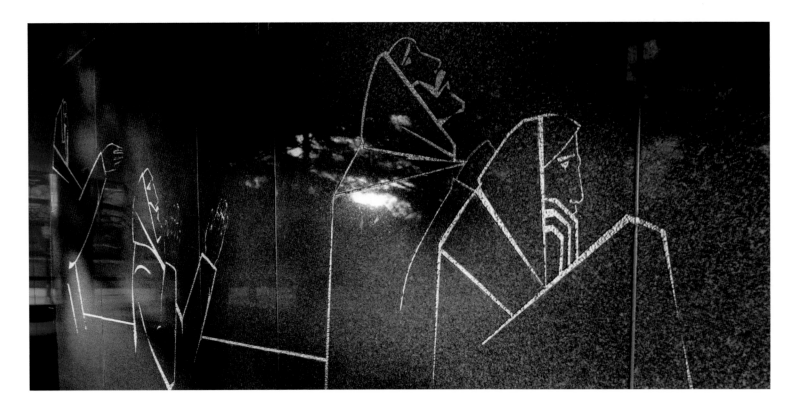

with gold, depict "symbols of Christ" that appear in Holy Scripture. This walking tour is an interesting one, connecting—like the *Word of Life* mural—ideas from both the Hebrew and Christian Scriptures.

The University of Notre Dame Archives do not reach deeply into the origins of this part of the "art program," but they do contain a little book, *Symbols of Christ,* written by Damsus Winzen, O.S.B., in 1955 and published by P. J. Kenedy & Sons. This humble document describes most of the symbolic images seen around the Library walls.

From the Hebrew Scriptures, the strolling Library visitor can ponder such symbols as the Burning Bush, the Key of David, and the Star of Jacob. Using references from the New Testament, figures also include the Precious Pearl, the Lamb of God, and the Bread of Life. The images are striking and yet simple, but the theological messages that accompany them, connecting them all to Christ, can be profound, even poetic.

For example, the reflection about Moses and the Burning Bush, based upon the reference in Exodus 3:2–3, goes like this: "The burning bush of the Old Testament represents not only the presence of God in the Old Testament and the permanence of life, but prefigures the incarnation, crucifixion, and resurrection of Christ—the new Moses—who is burning with life and the grace of the Holy Spirit."

These explanatory reflections are not inscribed alongside the images, but they are available on the Hesburgh Libraries website, and many of them are contained in an Office of Stewardship Programs publication, *Libraries: Collections and Services.* The introduction to the publication, written by University President Rev. John I. Jenkins, C.S.C., points to one "particularly apt" symbol in the granite—a simple cross engraved in a block.

This is Christ as cornerstone, Father Jenkins comments. He addresses benefactors reading the book: "It is on that cornerstone that this Library and, in fact, the entire University have been built, with the assistance of men and women like you who believe that Notre Dame's distinctive combination of scholarly excellence with religious faith and moral purpose offers hope for a world deeply in need."

He also recalls Father Ted's promise to benefactors of the 1960s that "what will happen here [in the Library] will in some small measure affect the world and all its problems." Father Jenkins goes on to say: "We strive not only to give our students knowledge, but to imbue them with a sense of transcendent purpose and a desire to use their education in service to a more just and humane world. You might call this a cornerstone of our mission."

Near the western entrance to the Library, there is one more religious image that echoes the building's homage to truth-seeking as a human enterprise with sacred significance. The image that welcomes patrons is an eighteen-foot-high statue of Moses holding the Ten Commandments.

Fides et Lectio

80

Holding those tablets with his left hand, Moses is angrily stomping on the golden calf that the Hebrew people had crafted as a false idol, and his right hand is pointing to heaven to remind his people that the one real God is Yahweh.

Is the "idol" mind a mischief-maker's workshop? This Moses reminds observers that the human cleverness that prompted people to nickname the mural "Touchdown Jesus" was hardly an isolated incident. Wags who sought to emphasize Father Ted's frequent departures from campus to attend high-level meetings joked that the statue of Moses pointing skyward simply was saying, "There goes Father Hesburgh!" As reported by *Notre Dame Magazine,* other students obviously liked to attribute football symbolism to works of art on campus, so they later gave Moses an enduring name by imagining that his raised index finger simply meant, "We're Number One." The patriarch's nickname was later revised more humbly to "First-Down Moses." The bronze statue of Moses, created by Joseph Turkalj, is a reminder of Ivan Mestrovic, Notre Dame's beloved artist-in-residence, who died in 1962 while the Memorial Library was being built. Mestrovic himself found Moses to be a compelling subject— an appropriate part of the Library's "art program." A Moses statue by Mestrovic, dating from the 1950s, has been on display on the second floor of the Library.

Metrovic's influence lives on through the work of thirty-nine-year-old Turkalj, whom Mestrovic had invited to come to Notre Dame as his assistant. Turkalj had worked with his fellow Croatian, Mestrovic, for five years, according to a *South Bend Tribune* article by John Mulvihill. Mestrovic, an internationally famous sculptor, had become resident artist at Notre Dame in 1955, with a studio built especially for him. When Mestrovic died at the age of 78, the University invited Turkalj to submit his own ideas for the Moses statue, and he received the commission for the project.

By the summer of 1963, the artist, who had been working in Mestrovic's studio, was ready to send a plaster mold of the huge image, cut into three sections, to Rome to be cast as a bronze statue. The newspaper article, published in February 1964, predicted that the statue would be back in South Bend in a few months, in time for the May dedication.

Meanwhile, the ultimate location for the statue became a point of contention, according to the *Tribune*. The original plan was to position Moses in the front of the Library, perhaps in the courtyard, presumably facing south, but this was "ruled out by an architect who thought the statue would distract from a mural on the building." Turkalj was quoted as saying the architect chose the west side of the building, where indeed the statue has taken up permanent residence, facing the central "God Quad," although the sculptor "designed the statue for an open area where it could be seen from all sides."

Fides et Lectio

The architectural firm of Ellerbe and Company may not have been contemplating the site of the new Library as "holy ground," in the words that the Burning Bush conveyed to Moses, but the project certainly did constitute fertile ground for the company's own self-expression and its own growth. The relationship between Ellerbe and Company and the University of Notre Dame, which had begun in the early 1950s with such buildings as O'Shaughnessy Hall, extended through to the renovation of the Main Building, completed in 2000.

Ellerbe went through some renovations of its own. The firm had become Ellerbe Becket through a merger in 1987. Then, in 2009, Ellerbe Becket was acquired by AECOM, a massive global company that had been formed from the engineering subsidiary of Ashland Oil in 1990 and had grown to have 44,000 employees around the world. AECOM provides technical and management services to construction and design projects in transportation, facilities, energy, and the environment.

By 2011, Ellerbe Becket, which called itself an architecture, interiors, and engineering firm, began operating exclusively as AECOM. Such a transition into an all-purpose global corporation was inevitable, says Thomas Dickmann, vice president of corporate communications for AECOM, based in New York. Things were simpler back in the 1960s at a place like Notre Dame—and Dickmann should know. He is a Domer who graduated in 1969 as an engineering major. He remembers the Memorial Library as a new and exciting feature of the campus.

"When you went into that building, it was almost like going into Disneyland," Dickmann recalls. "It was impressive as all get-out. You just knew you were in a wow-type building. I think it was the biggest building I had been in so far my whole life." Also, as an engineering major, he found the place useful. "I spent more hours in the Library than probably any other building on campus. It was quiet, with a great atmosphere, a real gathering place, with everything you needed."

Did the religious "art program" that Ellerbe had fashioned for the building, with the mural and the symbols of Christ and the Moses statue, seem odd at the time? "It was not out of place at all," he recalls, at least partly because so many Notre Dame students had gone to parochial schools and "the Catholicism and symbols weren't anything out of the ordinary."

By the way, Dickmann says he recalls the "Touchdown Jesus" moniker being "a phrase that was thrown about" during his years in the class of 1969, but he agrees that for the most part "it was more like a private joke" than a ubiquitous name for the mural.

Dickmann's office pointed out that a book called *The Ellerbe Tradition: Seventy Years of Architecture and Engineering* sheds light on that firm's unusual openness to artistic innovation at the time of the Memorial Library's inception. This written history of the company, drawn from the papers of Thomas Farr Ellerbe, FAIA, who headed the firm between 1921 and 1966, acknowledges that modernists of the period generally agreed with architect Adolf Loos's maxim, "Ornament is crime." But Ellerbe disagreed with this approach, taking a stance well-suited to Father Ted's approach to the library project. Notre Dame was inclined to add a second voice to the modernist message.

"Ellerbe had long professed a tradition of programmatically and structurally integrated ornament," according to the collection of personal papers. The company established a formal "art with architecture" program when it determined to add "human elements" in its design for the Mayo Clinic diagnostic center in Rochester, Minnesota, in the 1950s. The plan called for two large bronze statues outside and nine murals on the inside, all united around the theme, "Mirror to Man." This contrarian endeavor, embracing humanistic ideals and welcoming decoration as a friend of functionality, was the project that brought Ellerbe and Sheets together.

Ellerbe created about fifty "art programs" for various clients during the 1950s and 1960s. One seemed particularly noteworthy. "The 11-story granite mural of Christ that covered one façade of the Notre Dame Memorial Library was designed by Millard Sheets and supervised by [Ellerbe's in-house art consultant Warren] Mosman," reports *The Ellerbe Tradition*. "It was another example of Ellerbe's effort to incorporate art with architecture."

Some buildings integrate art and architecture in a way more appealing to modernists than the combination approach that produced Memorial Library. One can draw that conclusion from the comments of Duncan Stroik, an associate professor of architecture at Notre Dame and an internationally known expert in classical and sacred architecture.

"The architecture *is* the art," Stroik says of modernist sensibilities. In the 1960s, the modernist message about progress, as conveyed through structures like the Memorial Library, was one of bigness—form inspired more by functionality than by humanity. But Father Ted succeeded in building a symbol of Notre Dame's commitment to progress and the future while adding a mural that did celebrate humanity—and Christianity alongside. Additions like *The Word of Life* and the symbols of Christ "would have been very uncomfortable for most modern architects," says Stroik.

Today, at least on college campuses, modernist architecture is no longer seen as *de rigueur* to symbolize a commitment to progress. There is a renewed comfort level with traditional architecture, particularly neo-Gothic and Collegiate Gothic, and this has certainly been the pattern at Notre Dame, Stroik points out. Along with the university's ongoing commitment to new knowledge and human enlightenment, there has also been a return to religious symbolism and iconography on some buildings, with the Eck Hall of Law being a prime example.

Stroik opines with a smile that the combination of big, sparse architecture and big, traditionalist art arguably puts the Memorial Library "over the top." Then again, it might be seen as

yet another way in which the building forges connections between contrasts and thereby creates a fresh idea.

"What if we designed a library today?" Stroik asks rhetorically. "I think it would be traditional, or traditional-ish. It might be neo-Gothic, like Yale's new residential colleges. And we would have some iconography on it."

Clearly, a library built at Notre Dame today would not look like the Memorial Library, which is "very 1960s," as Stroik puts it. The Memorial Library does not stand as a contemporary benchmark of beauty for the university's consistently beautiful campus. But there's still something that makes the building a benchmark, or at least a landmark.

"I ask my students about it: Do people call the Library beautiful?" comments Stroik, who teaches Notre Dame architecture students about buildings with enduring beauty. "They say no, but it is what it is—a symbol of the university."

And that's quite enough to make a building enduring.

Chapter Three
TREASURES

The story of the Memorial Library now shifts inward, from the treasures one sees on the body of the building, from its exterior and from its earliest days, to the treasures that constitute the heart of the building—the people, places, and offerings that were and are organic parts of day-to-day life.

If the outside of the building spoke of the university as a community at a crossroads, the interior of the building was home to a cross-section of that community. It naturally included the university's faculty and students, as well as the Libraries' own faculty. This place later became a home of sorts for its founder, Father Ted. And, from the start, it has strived to serve up, for all the generations and branches of this family, the comforts of home—a place for interaction and information, for rest and renewal, and a place to feed the mind and the imagination, to cherish and share the things of enduring value. The concept of "library as place" is much-discussed in the field of library and information science, but Notre Dame's library has its own unique way to express it—in the flesh and bone behind the mural and stone.

A CITY OF SCHOLARS

The Memorial Library was designed to be convenient for students, but one might say the convenience of university faculty members was one of its "foundational" goals: the new building's basement was largely given over to office space for approximately two hundred professors, mostly from the College of Arts and Letters and the College of Business. The collection of faculty offices, arrayed along a series of parallel hallways, did provide privacy with doors and ceiling-to-floor walls, but, as one faculty member put it, "most of the occupants worked with their doors open, which made for a rather noisy environment, since all the furniture was metal. The sounds of ringing telephones, banging drawers, and scraping chairs, voices, footsteps, etc., echoed off the walls."

Nevertheless, this labyrinth of office space answered the campus's pressing need for such space and was promoted as the ultimate in convenience for scholars conducting research—a base of operations with nearly instantaneous access to a tower full of

books. Faculty received keys that gave them twenty-four-hour entry, through a separate door, to their offices. "You could actually get lost down there," one library administrator acknowledged. One scholar called the set-up a "rabbit warren," although he conceded that the close quarters "did create a more interactive faculty."

"A lot of people found it very confining," says Rev. Thomas Blantz, C.S.C., who remembers the Library's early days as a history professor using those offices as well as a chief university archivist using more spacious facilities elsewhere in the building. "Some people didn't like being underground." But Blantz personally enjoyed the proximity to books and appreciated the adjacency to the faculty stenographic pool—a precomputer convenience of the 1960s that combined machines and people as the hardware and software of the time. "You had at least four typist-stenographers" in their own section of the lower level, Blantz recalls. A professor preparing a letter or journal article "could pick up your telephone and be connected to a dictating belt," a sort of recording tape. The professor would dictate the words, the stenographers would soon transcribe them, "and two hours later they would slip under your door a typed copy."

Amy Belke, on staff in LaFortune's Student Activities Office, provided her own memories of working in the Library basement. "I started working on campus in October of 1976 in the steno pool. . . . There were about six ladies in the department. We typed manuscripts and communications for the faculty in the Arts and Letters Department. . . . They would dictate from their offices to our Dictaphone recording center. We would pick up tapes and take them to our desks to type out their correspondence and manuscripts."

Newer technology eventually moved in. "I do remember when we got our first [word-processing] computers and had to build walls around one of our areas in order to house 'the brain' of the computer," recalls Belke. "'The brain' was about three feet wide and four feet high, and we had to slide big floppy disks into slots that ran the main program. Then, at our desks, we had the large desktop computers with the big monitors—although the screen area was small. We had to load our big floppy disks into our computers—the disks were about six by six inches. Back then, we had to type in all the coding for paragraphs, capitalization, bolding, etc."

There was another feature added on the lower level for the convenience of the faculty. A small cafeteria unofficially called "the Pit" sold sandwiches and other items in vending machines. "It had Formica tables, plastic seating, and rows of vending machines," recalls one faculty occupant. "A lot of the younger faculty members purchased or brown-bagged hurried lunches there between classes. It was a popular meeting place—and about the only place in the building where one could legitimately consume food and drink, which were banned from the stacks on the upper floors. In the evenings, the Pit was occupied primarily by students."

Most of the faculty offices were moved out of the lower level when Decio Hall was built (by Ellerbe Architects) in 1984, and professors moved up in the world to more private, windowed spaces. Fact is, the lower-level space was always envisioned as a temporary home for faculty. Its ultimate destiny, which is being fulfilled today along with a role as a comfortable gathering place for students, was to supply additional book storage capacity. Much of that capacity, enough to hold at least a half million books on a single floor of the building, came in the form of compact shelving—the type that can be compressed together without aisles for people until a book is needed and the patron turns a crank to open up space between the shelves. This was one of the features added when the Library essentially gutted and reconstructed the lower level in 2002–2003, removing vending machines and remainders of the faculty "rabbit warren." *Notre Dame Magazine* says the renovated lower level reopened for business in late August 2003.

Right from the start and to a lesser degree today, there have been a variety of offices elsewhere in the Library ensuring that faculty members—and staff—remained a constant presence. Academic endeavors of all sorts were allowed to set up shop in the Library because, having been built to hold at least two million books, it offered plenty of office space for many years.

The Library became the home of Notre Dame's internationally respected journal, *The Review of Politics.* The building hosted the Jacques Maritain Center, the Soviet and Eastern European

Studies Center, and the University of Notre Dame Press. Notre Dame's Department of Education, which downsized into a small set of specialized graduate-level programs before closing completely, was housed for a time in the Library.

Remarkably, there was an office for the study of artificial intelligence, headed by Prof. Kenneth Sayre, who is still a member of Notre Dame's Department of Philosophy faculty today. Sayre, in a 2012 interview, said his Philosophic Institute for Artificial Intelligence (PIAI), incorporated as part of Notre Dame's Center for the Study of Man in Contemporary Society, received substantial support from the National Science Foundation to study mechanical recognition of patterns, among other topics. His research in the 1960s yielded cutting-edge, almost futuristic-sounding books including *Philosophy and Cybernetics* and *Consciousness: A Philosophic Study of Artificial Intelligence.*

Thus, nearly from the start, the Library housed the same convergence inside its walls as it reflected in its outward design—an interdisciplinary mix of past, present, and future; a deep interest in the person as well as in science and in the rapidly emerging transformations of modern life.

Many of the original offices in the Library have been moved to other locations on campus as other buildings were built to offer them space and as the Library simply needed more space for books. But there are several units that still hold pride of place within the Library and contribute mightily to its roles as a crossroads and house of academic treasures.

One is Notre Dame's renowned Medieval Institute, with one of the largest contingents of scholars of the Middle Ages—studying the cultures, languages, and religions approximately spanning the fifth through fifteenth centuries—at any North American university. "Over sixty faculty medievalists, from a dozen different departments, create a vibrant, interdisciplinary, intellectual community that sponsors frequent speakers, conferences, and other events," according to the institute's website. Researchers from around the world are attracted to the Medieval Institute book collection—more than 100,000 volumes, largely though not entirely housed at the Institute's headquarters on the seventh floor of the Library and considered one of the Hesburgh Libraries' world-class special collections.

Father Ted is especially proud of the agreement that he reached with Giovanni Batista Cardinal Montini (the archbishop of Milan, who became Pope Paul VI) for Notre Dame to house nearly the complete holdings, on microfilm, of Milan's Ambrosiana Library. The Ambrosiana is rich in Latin, Greek, Hebrew, Arabic, and vernacular resources from the Middle Ages, according to the Institute. The Frank M. Folsom Microfilm and Photographic Collection consists of positive and negative microfilms of over 10,000 medieval and Renaissance manuscripts belonging to the Ambrosiana Library, together with about 50,000 photographs of miniatures, illuminated initials, and drawings of European artists, supplemented by some 15,000 color slides. The Hesburgh

Libraries maintain a website devoted to the Medieval Institute Library and a link to the Ambrosiana Library.

The Memorial Library, upon its completion in 1963, immediately became the new home of another important set of historical holdings—the University of Notre Dame Archives. Occupying a large part of the sixth floor, the archives are focused primarily on safeguarding the permanent records of the university. The records span all academic and administrative offices, as well as persons and organizations conducting university business, plus the life of the student body as reflected in such publications as the *Scholastic* magazine, the *Observer* newspaper, and the *Dome* yearbook.

But the collection doesn't stop there. Notre Dame's archives contain extensive records "relating to the history of the Catholic Church and its people as lived in the American context," as the archives' website puts it. The Catholic collection, begun in the nineteenth century, "is recognized as one of the nation's foremost archival repositories for the study of American Catholicism. Major subject areas include Catholic publishing, higher education, social action, laity, and clergy."

Other collections in the University Archives contain the personal records of people associated with the university, including faculty, staff, alumni, and other supporters. The archives also contain over one million photographs or images—in prints, negatives, slides, and digital formats. The items on file in the archives also contain a growing number of audio and video files.

A CENTER FOR STUDENTS

Right from the start, the university's leaders saw the Memorial Library as a place for fellowship as well as scholarship. Faculty members and researchers from the campus and beyond would have abundant space for their work, but for the students this was to be a place of community that, you might say, put the "home" in "homework."

Victor Schaeffer, director of libraries at the time of the building's opening, boasted in a 1964 article how students were already flocking to the Library as part of their day's activities. "Surveys taken daily indicate that as many as 5,300 students—of the total student enrollment of 6,802—have used the Library on a particular day, and that at a particular hour, 1,352 users have entered the Library. The recorded book use has increased nearly 200 percent" from the patterns of the 1917 University Library, he reported in *Pioneer,* a magazine published by Remington Office Systems (suppliers of library equipment and furnishings). The magazine also noted that the Library could seat 3,000 people at a time. While touches of marble, walnut, and oak paneling were intended to make the entire setting comfortable and inviting for people, pockets of space with

comfortable seating for people were scattered among the shelves to encourage them to sit and read for a while.

"The first two floors of the building comprise the College Library," Schaeffer continued. "This area . . . provides facilities used by undergraduate and graduate students in normal course preparation and independent research. The College Library accommodates 2,411 readers—approximately 800 of whom are provided with individual tables and study carrels at one time. It also provides group study rooms, typing rooms, and stereophonic audio systems with headsets." The tower offered room for about four hundred students—graduate students for the most part—to read at any one time.

As time passed, the distinction between undergraduate space and graduate student space became less important. Indeed, in the early 1980s, the entire separation between the "College Library" and the "Research Library" was abandoned. At that point, the competition for a

comfortable reading space extended to everyone all at the same time, recalls James Neal, who was assistant director of the libraries at the time.

"The Library itself was a heavily used facility, and it continues to be the case," he says. "It was most aggressively used in the evenings. I remember vividly how students would come from dinner in the dining halls and pile into the Library at night. So it was very common that all the seats would be taken."

During the 1960s and 1970s, the arrangement of books into specialized mini-departments, with humanities primarily on the first floor and social sciences generally on the second floor, was meant to make basic research easier for undergraduates—without precluding the option for them to "dig more deeply" into a subject by entering the "Research Library" in the tower. "The undergraduate student, if he is capable of working with research materials, is encouraged to use the research collections," said Schaeffer.

Today, it's assumed that every student should and can gain access to the full panoply of information that is available throughout the library, and indeed throughout the world via the

Internet. The Library today—now, as flagship of the Hesburgh Libraries network spanning the campus—devotes more time to empowering students to navigate a sea of information that no single tower could hope to contain.

Librarians are on hand right from the start of the information journey for students in Notre Dame's College of the First Year of Studies. A self-guided introduction to the libraries called "Pot of Gold" is available at library.nd.edu. Students in Writing and Rhetoric courses receive an in-person introduction to the Hesburgh Libraries and their resources, along with guidance for creating a research strategy and evaluating information sources critically, according to librarian Sherri Jones, program director for academic outreach and engagement. She oversees the librarians who reach out to the first year students through classroom instruction and individual research consultation.

Is there anything that today's information-saturated generation doesn't feel comfortable pursuing? "The one thing the students feel the most uncomfortable about is just finding a book," says Jones. "They feel overwhelmed by the physical size of the Library." Many have never been in a library the size of the Hesburgh Library, and they underestimate the number of titles it contains—not only does it contain roughly three million books, it provides access to about the same munber of items in non-book form. But Jones says the students get their "sea legs" by going into the stacks as part of a book-finding exercise, and they emerge more knowledgeable and confident.

The help for newcomers doesn't end there. Indeed, it physically goes forth from the Library in the form of two "first-year experience" librarians. One holds office hours in the Coleman-Morse Center, and the other in O'Shaughnessy Hall, hoping to be just steps away from students when research-related questions arise. It's part of a new concept called "embedded librarians," explains Jones.

During an undergraduate's senior year, with an intensive independent research project quite possibly looming, the embedding can go in the opposite direction, one might say. Seniors can participate in a "thesis camp"—an intensive week-long experience headquartered on the lower level of the Hesburgh Library where librarians once again strive to resolve any mysteries of the information universe. In this case, "subject librarians," who are experts in the fields relevant to each student's thesis project, are on hand to offer advice on such important steps as creating a comprehensive literature review. There's even a similar "dissertation camp" for graduate students.

What do graduate students think of the Library these days? Mary C. Young, who departed from Notre Dame with a master's degree in early Christian studies in 2012 (and who happens to have been the research assistant for this book), tells this story:

When I decided to come to Notre Dame for graduate school, all of my professors at [un-dergraduate alma mater] Fordham kept speaking about how amazing the library at Notre Dame was—that it would be an invaluable resource to me and was one of the best in the country. I remember specifically the reflection of a professor who had been a visiting scholar there. She said, "You won't notice all of the snow because you'll be spending all of your time in that big, amazing, ugly library."

It's not the most beautiful building I've ever been in, but from the first time I set foot in it I knew that it was committed to making scholarship easy, modern, and excellent. When graduate students asked that articles only available in print be scanned upon request and emailed to the students, the request was granted [in good time]. When graduate students asked that books be requested online and then held in a centrally available location, it was granted. It would be hard to exaggerate how much easier this made gathering books and materials; hours could be lost among the stacks looking for the necessary books or scanning articles. With this method you could request materials in an exhausted haze at 1:30 a.m. and come in the next morning at 10 a.m. and pick up all of the books that you requested. Your articles would be emailed to your inbox!

More than the modern convenience of the library was the sense of mutual camaraderie and scholarship I felt with my fellow graduate students, be it in the tenth-floor graduate student reading room, the seventh-floor Medieval Institute reading room, or in the twelfth-floor theology reading room. The sense of mutual inquiry, hard work, and standard graduate school exhaustion made the library central to my experience in graduate school. Even now, it feels strange to leave work at the end of the day and not head into the windowless library for the next five hours. I will always remember and appreciate my time in that "amazing, ugly library."

Most undergraduates encounter the people, as well as the resources, of the Hesburgh Libraries regularly, in a variety of ways, throughout their four years. Some of the encounters will be in facilities other than the flagship building, such as formal instruction on specialized research for business students or chemistry majors. Virtually everyone needs help now and then, and the faculty and staff of the Hesburgh Library enjoy being just as available as the books that surround them, says Jones. When the need for help can indeed be responded to virtually, students use the "Ask the Librarian" service—a kind of chat room on the website.

"There's just so much information now, it can be overwhelming," she says. One particular service that librarians can provide is helping a student to determine "what's authoritative and what's not."

Sometimes, students are less interested in an authoritative source or a professional guide and more intent upon getting together with each other for collaboration or simple conversation. The Hesburgh Library continues to provide plenty of group study rooms for those purposes, too.

The Library's lower level was renovated in 2002 and 2003, removing all the old offices and adding high-tech compact shelving and attractive booths and tables for student seating. The new comforts opened the possibility for more congenial student gatherings, but the Library did not try to dictate the outcome. "The students themselves turned that into a quiet area," says Jones, pointing out yet another important purpose for the Library. Renovations of the first floor information-desk area several years later led to more talkative encounters among students, their professors, and the librarians. As of this writing, other renovations were going on to create a range of spaces, envisioning different kinds of meetings and mingling and technology-enhanced experiences, allowing different uses to spring up and spread out organically.

One constant of the Library's life is as predictable as the end of every semester. When final exams and term-paper deadlines approach, the Library becomes literally a round-the-clock crossroads for students with some serious studying to do. Finals week is a time when the Library "cuts some slack" for students who find unconventional ways to adopt the building as their personal study hall. "I can tell you all sorts of stories," says Ross Fergerson, manager of the department of building services. Students have found nooks and crannies in the building to set up shop with sleeping bags and small stockpiles of food and drink.

With this much interaction between students and the Hesburgh Library, it is inevitable that a certain amount of bonding occurs. There have been times when the students have overstepped the boundaries of that relationship, meeting university resistance, as with drinking games or the "bun run" tradition in which streakers dart through a section of the second floor during finals week.

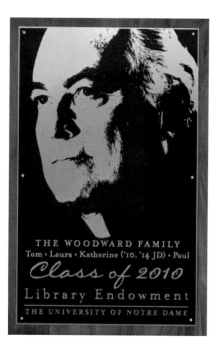

But one of the strongest signs of students bonding with the intellectual heart of the university is a long-term commitment of which Notre Dame can be proud. The Class of 2010 voted that their Senior Legacy, their collective gift to the university, would go to the Class of 2010 Hesburgh Libraries Endowment Fund. The fund, supported also by class parents Thomas and Laura Woodward, will exist in perpetuity to assist the acquisition of books, journals, and a spectrum of resources for future Library patrons.

"The Library did win most of the votes from the senior class, and I think it definitely makes a statement about the interests of our class," said Emily Everett '10, co-chair of the class development committee, quoted in *Access,* the Hesburgh Libraries newsletter. She noted the special value of contributing to the Library "because all Notre Dame students will use it."

Everett, who was a major in the Program of Liberal Studies, said the gift resonated with her own experience. "I personally spent a great deal of time in the Library. I have also found that the people who work in the Library are very friendly, willing to help, and knowledgeable. It's always been a great place for me to focus on the academic portion of my college career."

A PLACE FOR PROFESSIONALS

While many people today are approaching information as a readily available (even cheapened) commodity and deem libraries to be remnants from a pre-Internet past, Everett is right to have stressed the value of knowledgeable and helpful library professionals as indispensable for effective

learning today. Professionals of that sort were the lifeblood of the Memorial Library when it opened in 1963, and that has remained true for fifty years. What's more, the Library developed its own community, with its own unique cast of characters, and memories are still being made—and recalled with a smile—to this day.

The complete list of noteworthy contributors to the Library community is too huge to consider in this book, but one recollection about a classic character will suffice to show that this building was and is full of great stories. Microfilm was a technology spreading quickly in libraries during the 1950s and 1960s, especially valuable in preserving images from newspapers and other documents that were deteriorating. The Memorial Library acquired its own microfilmer-in-residence, a man named Frank Clark.

"When I first came to work at Notre Dame in 1973, there he was," recalls Katharina Blackstead, a Notre Dame librarian since 1973 who served the libraries as director of advancement for twenty years before retiring in 2012. "He was a uniquely interesting person in the strangest kind of way"—living alone, without the support of relatives, apparently raised amid financial and educational disadvantages, with a cigarette perpetually hanging out of his mouth. "He had a love of books, of learning, and of Catholicity in all its manifestations. He had a passion for maintaining the record of the American Catholic experience." Clark had his office on the lower level, where he transferred countless documents to microfilm throughout the 1960s and 1970s. Even after many university faculty members had abandoned their basement offices in favor of grander spaces in Flanner Hall and elsewhere, Clark remained—a bit of a "hermit," as one former colleague put it. "He had quite a setup down there, and he worked odd hours," recalls Blackstead. Members of the Library community befriended Clark, and he returned the favor with both loyalty and interesting conversation.

In 1983, Jeffrey M. Burns wrote a history of Notre Dame's Cushwa Center for the Study of American Catholicism. The center continued to benefit from the Memorial Library's Catholic Americana Collection, he pointed out. As quoted in the Library's *Access* newsletter in 2004, Burns said this:

At the heart of the Center's collection program in the early years was the late Francis P. Clark (1936–1979). Clark, head of the University Microfilming Department since the early 1960s, was assigned to direct the Center's collection and development program. Mr. Clark had an uncanny knack for finding valuable materials hidden away amidst apparently insignificant rubbish. His own personal collection of Catholic Americana rivaled that of many libraries, and Frank willingly shared his collection with any interested scholars. The most significant of Clark's efforts was the microfilming of American Catholic newspapers from across the country. As a result of his work, Notre Dame now maintains one of the most extensive collections of Roman Catholic newspapers on film available anywhere in the United States. . . . As one obituary read, "His untimely death has left a void in the American Catholic scholarly community that will never adequately be filled."

This was one story of a diamond in the rough constituting a treasure for the Memorial Library, and later for American Catholicism. But the story of people who preserved the building's treasures goes on and now enters its sixth decade.

During those first fifty years, only six people held leadership as director of libraries. Victor A. Schaefer was at the helm during the crucial time of transition between the 1917-vintage library and the new building. His successors were Rev. James W. Simonson, C.S.C., in 1966, David E. Sparks in 1971, Robert C. Miller in 1978, Jennifer A. Younger in 1997, and Diane Parr Walker in 2011. Regretfully, it is beyond the scope of this book to discuss each director's significant

impacts on the Hesburgh Libraries and the university as a whole, but more information about them is available in *What is Written Remains,* in the libraries' online *Access* newsletter archives, and on the university's website.

All of these directors have had to manage through periods of great change for the libraries, for the university, and for information professionals. Joanne Bessler, organizational development librarian, says the job descriptions and expectations for those who work for the Hesburgh Libraries—numbering approximately 170 as of summer 2012, up from about 60 when the Memorial Library opened—have been transformed by changes in publishing, scholarly communication, information technologies, library science, and by faculty and student desires.

"Library users just aren't what they used to be," she wrote in *Access* in 2003. "Although researchers still seek information from authoritative sources and thrill at the chance to use special collections, they want most information presented, packaged, and delivered in customized ways. They expect electronic articles, videos, manipulable data, images, books, and hand-held computer screens." These changing expectations "have radically altered the composition of the Libraries' staff" and have transformed individual roles and expectations.

Today's library users independently can find huge quantities of information on most topics, Bessler acknowledges. "But they rely on the Library for expertise in locating and accessing unique, authoritative, and highly specialized resources—and for providing seamless access to resources regardless of format or location." This prompts the Library to continue expanding its knowledge pool, upgrading the expectations for nearly every position, and recruiting additional experts.

Bessler offered a helpful comparison for this book: "In 1963, an employee in an entry level staff position was expected to check materials in and out using paper records, clip articles from newspapers to mount on paper and to file in vertical files, and to file thousands of catalog cards and patron records, insert updated pages in time-sensitive reference books, and shelve books." In contrast to staff positions, "librarians handled collection development, acquisitions, reference, cataloging, and management. Their expertise was in finding information and resources since indexes were in paper format, infrequently cumulated, and often non-existent."

The scene is different in 2012: "Today's entry level staff members need to master multiple technologies and activities," Bessler explains. Some staff members perform responsibilities once done by librarians. Administrative and technology professionals contribute expertise in such areas as "budget and facilities administration, web development, systems, digital initiatives, instructional technology, and programming." Meanwhile, the Library faculty has grown in size and expertise. Librarians have been recruited to add expertise in East Asian studies, Latin paleography and manuscript studies, digital programs, digital access, resource licensing, and metadata creation. Although the Hesburgh Libraries have always been service oriented, there is a new commitment to integrate library planning and resources with priorities and goals all across campus, Bessler says.

The *sine qua non* for a librarian is to provide excellent professional service, adds Blackstead, and librarians "have the responsibility to provide vision and leadership in helping to chart the future direction of the libraries." Many people do not know that the librarians of the Hesburgh Libraries (and of the separate Kresge Law Library) have faculty status—not sharing the exact same category as the university's teaching and research faculty, more commonly termed university faculty, but still given faculty recognition and responsibilities according to the university's guidelines. Not unlike the faculty members in the various academic colleges, disciplines, and departments, Library faculty are called upon to direct their service locally, nationally, and globally, one might say. They are accountable to their Notre Dame colleagues and stakeholders to fulfill their duties on campus, even as they are accountable for the ongoing endeavors of their disciplines and their profession.

That accountability can take many forms. The Hesburgh Libraries are part of a dynamic community of libraries around the country. Library faculty members from Notre Dame contribute to that community through leadership of and service on national or regional committees of groups like the American Library Association (ALA) and the Special Libraries Association (SLA).

They may be called upon to assist in the work of the Association of Research Libraries (ARL), a selective group that deals directly with the head librarians at its member institutions. Synergy with these professional groups is an important part of a library's standing in the professional and academic community. It was only in 1962, with the Memorial Library under construction, that the thirty-year-old ARL admitted the University of Notre Dame as a member, deemed worthy of its mission to "develop and increase the resources and usefulness of the research collections in American libraries." Still today, the ARL has invited only about 125 libraries into membership.

Aside from contributions to the most prestigious national organizations, library faculty members may get involved in smaller projects related to statewide or local initiatives, for example, or overarching matters of professional values, such as privacy and censorship concerns. They also compose articles for peer-reviewed journals based on independent research. Their associations and contributions off-campus earn Notre Dame librarians their share of honors and recognition from their peers around the country.

"The implicit concept is excellence," says Blackstead. "One's collaborations with peers in the profession and engagement with the major issues in the rapidly changing world of information enhance one's leadership and service at Notre Dame, and it's a virtuous feedback loop. The faculty title symbolizes professional librarians bringing visibility to Notre Dame while also bringing Notre Dame's expertise and values to librarianship in the United States and around the globe." It also highlights the opportunity for Library faculty and other university faculty to work together as peers—everyone nurturing the life of the mind for the sake of the student.

Notre Dame has its own award for excellence in the field of library and information science. The Rev. Paul J. Foik, C.S.C., Award is given annually to a library faculty member "who has contributed significantly to library service to the Notre Dame community or to the library profession through personal scholarship or involvement in professional associations." Father Foik was a Holy Cross priest who served as director of Notre Dame's library from 1912 to 1924, during the move of the Lemonnier Library from the Main Building to the University Library, which opened in 1917. He was also a national leader in the library profession of his time. (Sherri Jones, Joanne Bessler, Katharina Blackstead, and Maureen Gleason, all previously mentioned in this book, are among the Foik Award winners.)

TREASURE ON THE THIRTEENTH FLOOR

He may not be a librarian, but Father Ted has continued to be a leading contributor to the Library as place, as community, as crossroads, and as a collection of memories that inform the future.

The very fact that the place exists is attributable to Father Ted, so it's not surprising that he came to feel especially at home in the Memorial Library after he retired as university president. He ended his thirty-five years of leadership in 1987, the longest-tenured university president in the United States, and he immediately wanted to see more of the world about which he cared so much. Father Ted, along with Father Ned, who retired as executive vice president at the same time, headed off on a year-long sabbatical journey of rest and intellectual renewal. That international adventure later resulted in the book *Travels with Ted and Ned*.

Father Ted explains what happened after those travels in another one of his books—his autobiography, *God, Country, Notre Dame*. "On my return, I found my old office desk, my books,

and, best of all, my secretary of almost forty years, Helen Hosinski, moved to the thirteenth floor of the newly named (I tried to avoid it) Theodore M. Hesburgh Library." After so many years in the center of the action, this priest wanted to feel the energy of the crossroads again, but he was happy to do it humbly. Despite Father Ted's argument that a place should not be named for someone until that person is deceased, the university trustees voted in 1987 that the Library should be renamed in his honor.

His love for the Notre Dame community and for his new office in the Library were inseparable: "My new office fulfilled all my desires," he wrote in the autobiography, "with bookshelves from floor to ceiling and a window giving the best possible panoramic view of the Notre Dame campus, with the Gold Dome and the Sacred Heart Church spire in the center." Evincing another inseparability, "Ned Joyce occupied the office adjacent to and similar to mine."

With Father Ted's move to the thirteenth floor complete, the next twenty-five years became a time for the Notre Dame family—and many others—to draw even closer to him. His office has attracted a steady stream of visitors. He also has welcomed dignitaries of all sorts up to the fourteenth-floor penthouse, with its wonderful views not only of the heart of the campus, but Notre Dame Stadium, as well. There's another special place he shares with guests—a small chapel in his office suite, where he has celebrated daily Mass, often with visitors. Football weekends have prompted premier opportunities for such celebrations, appropriately welcoming a deeper communion with the Christ pictured on the building's exterior.

Craig Horvath '88, director of reunion giving and volunteers for the university's annual giving programs, is one of many people with a big story from that small chapel. He recalls that, when his uncle John Monhaut passed away in 2003, after having worked twenty years for Notre Dame as a maintenance supervisor, Father Ted agreed to offer a Mass for him, with the entire Monhaut, Kramer, and Horvath family present, in the thirteenth-floor chapel. Craig was given a special blessing in Father Ted's private office and was called upon to assist him, first in vesting and then during Mass as a reader and extraordinary Eucharistic minister. "It was an amazing and humbling honor and a lasting memory, and it made me feel an even closer part of the Notre Dame family," Horvath recalls. "And it touched all of us that my aunt Agnes, who had been an office manager for over twenty years, for support services for the university, and my uncle, who moved tables and chairs for the university, were valued members of the Notre Dame family in the heart of this great priest and leader of the family."

As of this writing, although age and failing eyesight have taken their toll, Father Ted has shifted largely from world traveler to campus presence. He still could be found at a variety of events in 2013, including his seventieth jubilee as a Holy Cross priest and at other occasions

where the inspiration of Notre Dame's elder statesman is appreciated by alumni and new-comers alike.

He has continued to stay well-informed and interested in an array of issues. Every day, he receives assistance from students who read newspapers and other texts to him, and he has retained the caring heart of a priest and pastor. He has continued to meet and correspond with leaders at all levels, while also exemplifying Holy Cross hospitality to members of the Notre Dame family and to visitors from all walks of life. As of fall 2012, Father Ted was welcoming guests and maintaining a seven-day-a-week presence in the Library.

Father Ted's indispensable aide in all of these efforts has been Melanie Chapleau, whose desk is the first stop for every visitor to his office. The role of traffic cop is important at such a busy intersection. "She's very good at that," Father Ted said in a 2012 interview, noting that the job of sentry and scheduler involves saying the occasional no. "She does it in a nice way . . . she kills them with kindness, but she's got standards." Chapleau has been his assistant for about a quarter of a century, succeeding Helen Hosinski upon the latter's retirement. "It's my luck that I've gone through all these years [as university president and president emeritus] with only two secretaries," said Father Ted in a 2012 interview. (He also added a thank-you to Pat Roth, whom he said was Father Ned Joyce's secretary for fifty years, both in the Main Building and the Library.) There's a very tangible thank-you to Hosinski in the Main Building. She is part of the Wall of Honor on the ground level.

The combination of awards, gifts, honors, photographs, and other memorabilia Father Ted has received, both during his presidency and during his retirement, has produced one of the Library's most fascinating collections, and much of it is displayed right in his office suite, for all visitors to see.

One large room, between the reception area and the chapel, has a particularly overwhelming collection of items. "It's a great room because it's full of memories," he told a visitor in 2011, pointing here and there. "Every one of these has a story." He touches a priceless urn given to him during a summer he spent in China during his presidency. It's "a reminder for me of my love for the Chinese people." He points to a photo of the Lockheed SR-71 Blackbird, a plane in which he was privileged to fly, as a rare civilian passenger, at more than three times the speed of sound.

Elsewhere in the suite, one finds the Presidential Medal of Freedom he received in 1964 and a Congressional Gold Medal he received in 2000. Photographs show him carrying the Olympic torch in 2002, shaking hands with presidents and other political leaders, as well as throwing out the first ball (along with Father Ned) at a World Series game in Yankee Stadium.

Father Ted's actual business office has been the site of many memorable handshakes and conversations. One alumnus remembers the light-hearted story that circulated in 1988 when

President Ronald Reagan visited Notre Dame to officially unveil a Knute Rockne postage stamp. According to this apocryphal anecdote, when Reagan visited Father Ted in his Library office and saw a red phone on his desk, Reagan reportedly remarked, "Father Ted, I have a phone like that on my desk, and I can use it to reach any national leader in the world. Who can you reach on your phone?" Father Ted quipped that his phone could reach God. Reagan said, "That must be a pretty expensive phone call, to reach God." Father Ted explained, "No. From Notre Dame, it's a local call."

Many of the more serious stories from that office are embodied in books on Father Ted's shelves, reflecting both the everyday work and the global concerns he has dealt with as president and president emeritus. Some of these books were written by him. Other volumes present his international travels or recall his work for the Civil Rights Commission and other forms of service. Of course, that service ranged widely, including not only Notre Dame, but the Vatican, the International Atomic Energy Agency, the Overseas Development Council, and more.

There's no room in the office for all the books that Father Ted has received over the years, but the Library has a place for those.

RAREFIED BUT REAL

"One special collection we have is all of Father Hesburgh's books," says Lou Jordan, head of the Department of Rare Books and Special Collections. "There are several thousand volumes that are all dedicated to him by people not only from Notre Dame but around the world. Presidents from Eisenhower on, many world leaders, famous scholars and scientists have all donated signed copies of their books." New additions to that collection continue to arrive in boxes from Melanie Chapleau.

That's just the beginning of the treasures found in Rare Books and Special Collections, a unit given a substantial amount of space in the design of the Memorial Library. The department is headquartered behind glass doors along the building's main concourse, but most of its collections are stored in the lower level. Jordan describes the extent of the holdings using several categories.

The "rare books" can be defined as books printed before 1830, a period when the hand-pulled printing press was replaced by mechanical presses that produced much larger quantities of a book, with standardized quality. A book might also qualify for the "rare" category by having a value around $3,000–$5,000 or higher, or by being of a peculiar size or having an unusual background.

Manuscripts are hand-written materials. Notre Dame's manuscript collection includes Babylonian clay tablets from 3000 BC, fragments of papyrus from Egypt, and items from the Middle Ages and modern day. As an example of more recent manuscripts, the Library holds many personal letters written during the Civil War, and the contents of these are being digitized for Internet viewing. Several history majors have used those collections for their senior theses.

Some "special collections" are noteworthy not because of the value of individual items within them, but because they are valuable as a comprehensive, complete unit. The G. K. Chesterton Collection, for example, contains over 2,000 books and periodicals by or about the prolific British Catholic author-journalist-poet. This assemblage of almost everything Chesterton ever wrote came from a Notre Dame alumnus in 1965.

The Joyce Sports Research Collection contains all sorts of printed materials related to sports, including 3,000 books, many magazines dating back to the 1700s, and "ephemera" such as record books, scorecards, programs, and media guides, according to Jordan. The collection also contains what librarians call "realia"—such as actual baseballs and gloves, not printed, but still valuable for research and nostalgia. Most of the collection, supported by an endowment in honor of avid sports enthusiast Father Ned Joyce, was built up before the 1970s. That provenance, pre-dating the years of explosive growth in sports collecting, helped to reduce the risk of invasion by counterfeits and to make the collection an enduring benchmark of authenticity, Jordan pointed out. There's nothing inauthentic about naming a world-class sports collection after Father Ned. He was a leader in college sports administration for years and played an influential role in making the National Collegiate Athletic Association (NCAA) a strong voice for academic integrity.

By the way, the sports collection is not the place to look for the history of Notre Dame's own sports activities. The University Archives hold a separate Notre Dame athletics collection. But the Library does happen to house all the records of a lesser known local sports phenomenon—the South Bend Blue Sox, one of the teams in the All-American Girls' Professional Baseball League. The national women's league existed in the 1940s and 1950s and served as the basis for the Hollywood film *A League of Their Own*.

Special collections in the Library cover a wide spectrum of subjects, but some of the world-class "destination collections" for which Notre Dame is best known include Catholicism, medieval studies, Dante, Byzantine studies, Irish studies, Latin American studies, colonial American numismatics, and the aforementioned sports resources.

Just as Notre Dame has been called the place "where the church does her thinking," it is fitting to think of Notre Dame as a place where the church in America does her remembering. There is a remarkable amount of Catholic Americana among the rare books. Catholic pamphlets constitute an abundant special collection—as do Catholic newspapers, thanks partly to microfilmer Frank Clark. But the roots of Notre Dame's Catholic collections go much farther back, to James F. Edwards, better known as Jimmie Edwards, a charismatic and pious man who directed Notre Dame's library from about 1873 to 1911. Edwards' passion was to build up a "Catholic Reference Library of America," and he largely succeeded through his vigorous outreach to bishops, Catholic historians, and others. According to Philip Gleason and Charlotte Ames in *What is Written Remains,* by 1911 Notre Dame already stood as "the nation's leading center of Catholic Americana." The Library's Catholic resources are complemented by extensive holdings on the sixth floor belonging to the University Archives.

Notre Dame's Medieval Institute draws upon an extraordinary collection centered on the Library's seventh floor. As mentioned above, the Library houses microfilm and photographic

copies of nearly all the holdings of the Ambrosiana Library in Milan, and the microfilms continue to be valuable back-up copies despite the rather old technology, says Jordan. To digitize all the unique manuscripts would be prohibitively expensive and time-consuming.

The Library has one of the finest Dante collections in North America, thanks largely to Rev. John Zahm, C.S.C., who purchased much of the material, including examples of very early printings and other rare editions, in 1902. One might say that Father Zahm, whose name is given to one of Notre Dame's residence halls, was a "Renaissance man" in more than one sense. Not only did he cherish Dante (who admittedly predated the Renaissance), but he built his academic reputation primarily as a scientist. He contributed significantly to the growth of the university's science museum. For good measure, this master of interdisciplinarity was an early contributor to the Library's well respected Latin American collections; he donated his personal library of books acquired during extensive travels in South America, including his participation in (ex-President) Theodore Roosevelt's 1913 scientific expedition on that continent.

All told, the special collections of Notre Dame contain many items worthy of display, recognition, and wonderment. The design of the Memorial Library sought to foster such appreciation with several different kinds of spaces. When one enters the Department of Rare Books and Special Collections from the main concourse, the first space is an exhibit room. Jordan notes that much attention is given to the exhibits of rare books, not only by his own staff but by the Hesburgh Libraries' outstanding experts in conservation and preservation. "A special book support is made for every book in an exhibit," says Jordan. Also, lighting is kept low in the exhibit room to protect the books.

Beyond the exhibit room, there is a long, classic reading room. That space and a separate seminar room host more than one hundred university classes and lectures every year. One never knows how the Libraries' special collections might be featured or celebrated. Jordan told of a recent occasion when a historic music manuscript, a centuries-old collection of the Psalms, was acquired and used in the Master of Sacred Music Program. The reading room temporarily became a singing room, one might say, when students gathered for a performance of the songs.

A smaller, glassed-off space near the reading room is the venue where the old manuscripts are actually presented to be viewed and handled by qualified visitors. The Library staff provide a watchful eye.

More than a thousand people make use of the special collections area every year, according to Jordan, and it's a pleasure to share their excitement at simply seeing or touching a book that connects them to history. "There's something for everyone," he says. A lawyer might especially enjoy a first-printing copy of the United States Constitution. A scientist might relish a first edition of Copernicus in which he posits that the Earth revolves around the Sun.

Protection of the Library's special treasures entails plenty of alarms, cameras, motion detectors, and other technology. Under the guidance of the Preservation Department, steps are also

taken to control temperature and humidity in the large special collections storage space downstairs. Preservation staff members, who do repairs on all damaged books, take extra pre-emptive steps for special collections, such as making storage boxes or covers for books.

Some holdings don't impose significant needs for technology, but a growing number of materials receive more than the usual security in place for the general collections. Jordan says many books nowadays are described as "medium rare" because they are at risk of being stolen. "More people have learned the value of books" over the past decade thanks to eBay and other phenomena. Jordan cites the example of travel guides dating back to the nineteenth century and describing various cities or states. These might not be valued at the price levels of "rare books," but they could be seen as desirable by collectors and hence deserving of lock-and-key, rather than open-shelf, storage.

Treasures

Notre Dame continues its commitment to special collections—both by adding new materials to existing collections and by establishing new collections. Much of this work is done by subject librarians, in consultation with colleges, departments, and individual scholars of the university. Storage of these additional volumes has been made easier by the fact that the renovation of the Hesburgh Library's lower level in 2001–2003 created significantly more space for special collections. The acquisitions are funded by university allocations or by the support of benefactors—a support which has been growing both in financial terms and in the level of engagement by scholars and students since the 1980s.

Indeed, there is nothing static about special collections, or library collections in general. As the university has embraced interdisciplinary research and collaboration more and more, the lines between collections have grown more permeable. There are more plentiful ties between special collections and the general collections on shelves and online. All of these connections can bear fruit for perceptive seekers.

A more rapidly changing world means that materials have to be acquired more quickly and managed more nimbly, offering scholars the resources needed for international peace studies or nanotechnology or various business trends. With digital technology, special collections have come to incorporate many more resources in forms other than hard-bound books, and they have to be accessible everywhere. As information availability explodes, decisions must be made about how much of a collection to retain at all or to have immediately on hand—and how much to store remotely for delivery to scholars and students "just in time" for their needs. As the university has sought to be on the cutting edge of research, more collections have been built up in areas of study that barely existed ten or twenty years ago.

One direction in which special collections is heading is symbolized by an "Initiative on the American Dream" that the libraries established in 2008 with the support of a generous family's endowment. It is built not around a single author, country, or field of study, but around a concept that has proven compelling to many people—including scholars—who see it through different lenses. The libraries, working first with the College of Arts and Letters but increasingly with other disciplines on campus, has been acquiring and linking resources from sociology, political science, economics, history, and American studies in forms such as DVDs, newspapers, digital assets, and books. Studies of what the American Dream has meant and might come to mean—among today's immigrant populations, for example—can lead to course offerings in departments, classes in the Library, fresh independent research, connections with science and entrepreneurship, and perhaps new hope.

"Suppose someone studying the American Dream comes up with something nobody has come up with before that *saves* the American Dream for future generations," comments Blackstead. "That's what the university may be enabling through its medical research and its research in critical technologies." It turns out that much of the university is, in some sense, exploring (perhaps even expressing) the American Dream—or an increasingly global version of it, like that glimpsed at the 1964 "Symposium on the Person in the Contemporary World"—but it takes the Library to bring all that information together around an idea.

The intertwined nature of these subject areas and research related to them makes the point that the entire collection of books and other titles in the Hesburgh Libraries—not merely the "special collections"—is worthy of recognition. Plenty of initiative and imagination have gone into building it and using it, and the same attributes will allow it to be used even more efficiently and effectively in the future.

PAYING IT FORWARD

In the midst of all the university's special collections, new research resources, state-of-the-art media, and springs of creativity, especially if one thinks of the Library as a crossroads where these can come together, it is helpful to recall the image of a single item that has stood in the middle of the main concourse since the Memorial Library opened in 1963.

It is the oddly attractive stanchion that supports a carousel of two dozen gold-laden panels. Each panel contains a long list of names to be browsed as an exercise of respect or simple curiosity. Two intersecting words top the stanchion: "Donors Honored." This tribute to people who contributed gifts for construction of the Memorial Library more than fifty years ago stands as a symbol of one crucial component yet to be pondered in this story.

"The Hesburgh Libraries have a number of treasures—the resources, the people, the services," says Katharina Blackstead, whose primary duties over the course of forty years involved outreach to benefactors. "Donors are an integral part of all these treasures. They tie together and make possible these treasures. Their caring for the libraries is a treasure in and of itself."

The stanchion, whose nearby companion piece is a more simply designed directory of the building, does not stand alone in its mission to honor generous contributors who make the Library

forever new. There is a decades-old legacy of commemorative plaques on walls throughout the building, thanking benefactors who contributed to constituent parts, large and small.

A growing assemblage of decorative golden plaques—now numbering more than 210—lines the walls of the main concourse, mostly but not entirely toward its eastern end. They represent diverse contributions, or "leadership gifts," that have been made to the university libraries, as well as the people behind those gifts.

Each plaque has its own unique character. It may represent a new "special collection" or a valued addition—either to a preexisting special collection being carefully reserved or to the vast selection of books in the open stacks. Those stacks may be in the Hesburgh Library or one of the branches of the Hesburgh Libraries or the Kresge Law Library. The materials represented by the plaques most often are books, but they could be newspapers or "realia" or other written, audio/ visual, or digital products. These resources could have been handed over to the university as the final fruits of someone's lifetime of passionate collecting in a favorite field of interest.

A plaque may represent someone's transfer of an intact collection or a monetary gift—totaling $100,000 or multiple millions of dollars—so that librarians could purchase, over time, more materials relevant to the theme of the collection. Portions of these leadership gifts might be earmarked to sponsor conferences and lectures or to sustain subscriptions to digital materials. There may be little or no earmarking: the Hesburgh Libraries increasingly invite gifts that are general endowments, not focused on a single subject or a narrow purpose, but available to be used nimbly in response to rapidly emerging information needs. Each plaque may be named in honor of an individual or family who made the donation, or it may carry the name of a figure who inspires others to give. The latter is true of the Rev. Edward A. Malloy, C.S.C., General Library Endowment, a general fund into which donations continue to flow.

There's one more way in which every plaque has its own personality. Each donor whose gift will be recognized on the concourse wall is invited to guide the design of a unique visual message. The design might represent people, places, or things that are important to the donor or relevant to the subject of the collection, or both. This results in plaques that are rich in meaning to the families of the generous givers—often as reminders of a person's love for books, for a vocation or avocation, or simply for alma mater Notre Dame.

The designs also result in enjoyable browsing by passersby. Just as the Library's outside walls contain "symbols of Christ," the interior concourse walls contain symbols from the minds and hearts of friends of Notre Dame. A number of the plaques contain images of the Grotto or "Touchdown Jesus"—that is, *The Word of Life*.

One among many examples of this phenomenon is the plaque symbolizing the Jolene and Anthony DiMaggio General Library Endowment. Its eye-catching image shows *The Word of Life* mural towering over Notre Dame Stadium with the scoreboard frozen at a moment in time from a particular football game in 1977. It shows the final score—Notre Dame 49; Southern California 19—of the famous "Green Jersey Game" in which Coach Dan Devine's Fighting Irish, wearing green jerseys, trounced arch-rival USC before going on to win a national championship.

These visual images and tributes to benefactors may be seen in places far beyond the Library's main concourse. They are archived at the university website, for example. Moreover, in many cases, the plaques have been reproduced as bookplates that adorn the inside cover of every book in a donated collection. Some of these bookplate images, or at least a note crediting the leadership gift, also can be seen accompanying the online listings of the donated resources, meaning that the medium and the message of a benefaction can now be seen around the world whenever someone is browsing the virtual bookshelves.

While the "Donors Honored" stanchion in the concourse—and the older golden commemorative plaques one sees all over the building—recall a time when contributors thought very concretely about every specific component of a grand new Memorial Library, benefactors increasingly have been encouraged to take a broader view of their support for learning. The physical building is just one place where a contribution can be seen. A collection of books about automobiles, for instance, may become inextricably linked—through computerized methods of access and through the insights of librarians and interdisciplinary thinkers at Notre Dame and around the world—to research about energy and the environment, about economics and suburbanization, and indeed about the American Dream.

Whereas benefactors fifty years ago needed to focus very practically on contributing the concrete, wood, and paper innards of a specific library building, donors today are often invited to focus, just as practically, on the resources, programs, and services that constitute everyday librarianship and information science. While donations of specific books and collections will always be welcome, assuming those resources are relevant to Notre Dame's wide spectrum of learning, benefactors are asked to think in terms of broader fields—science and engineering, humanities, social science, business, or arts and architecture—and how they might support the rapidly evolving scholarship within or across those fields.

The whole idea of contributing to the Library is evolving and expanding. Research and teaching faculty, departments, and colleges of the university are increasingly prone to collaborate with the Hesburgh Libraries and with library faculty; they see their mutual interest in prioritizing and securing the information resources needed to keep pace with developing knowledge. Financial support must come from a variety of sources, including the university as a whole. The office of President Rev. John Jenkins, C.S.C., has tapped the generosity of the President's Circle group of givers to expand the Library's holdings for such programs as sacred music and peace studies. The

University's new capital campaign, starting in 2013, is expected to highlight the need for general and specific gifts to the libraries, fostering not only the resources on the shelves but the programs and the services that bring the resources alive for people.

The magnitude of the information to be utilized and the learning to be nurtured these days might make the fifty-year-old stanchion of donors seem minimalist to many visitors today. The same could be said of the main concourse's other (often unnoticed) reminders of the Library's dedication—two golden doors, on either side of the inner sliding doors, that doubled as six-foot-tall dedication plaques. One door contains words recognizing the Ford Foundation's generosity to higher education in general and to Notre Dame in particular—generosity that supported the Library's construction. The other door has a commemorative message from the day of dedication. It reads: "May 7, 1964; Notre Dame Memorial Library: A Living Monument to the Devotion and Generosity of Thousands of Notre Dame Alumni and Friends; Theodore M. Hesburgh, C.S.C., President; Ellerbe Architects."

The stanchion, the dedication doors, and the rows of golden plaques are anything but trivial. They still remind everyone traversing the Hesburgh Library concourse that innumerable people—engaging their minds, hearts, and values—form the foundation of all the progress the Memorial Library was built to symbolize. The amazing amount of intellectual progress now embodied in the building goes nowhere unless it is received, utilized, and treasured by people—by the whole Notre Dame family.

Chapter Four
CHAPTERS OF CHANGE

Just as the main concourse's plaque-like door proclaims, the Hesburgh Library of today is a living monument. It has shared in fifty amazing years of life at Notre Dame, with all of the changes, challenges, and triumphs that such a lifespan suggests. In the spirit of Father Ned Joyce and Millard Sheets, who climbed the campus water tower in 1963 to assess the "big picture"—the past, present, and future—of the *Word of Life* mural, the life story of this iconic building now sweeps through time to consider where it has been and where it is headed.

A REAL PAGE-TURNER

The story of the Library's treasures has already allowed us to browse through the building's first five decades. Faculty members literally have come and gone from their central position on the lower level. Notre Dame's students have enjoyed all the comforts of home while experiencing the inevitable conflicts between the familiar shelves and the new digital frontier. Library professionals have seen their base of operations stay the same in many ways even as those operations changed rapidly and radically. Father Ted has treasured the Library and has

been treasured as a member of the Library community, sharing his diverse gifts with a community that spans the world. The Library's collections have grown in size, in variety, and in value. Donors have continued and expanded the tradition of generosity that made the building possible.

Against this backdrop, other scenes have been acted out.

One of the fundamental concepts steering the Library's design and the organization of its contents faded away in 1981. The "College Library," housed on the first two floors, and the "Research Library," housed in the tower, were merged. The dual approach that was deemed a sagacious innovation in the 1960s no longer made sense at a time when undergraduates, especially juniors and seniors, were behaving more and more like graduate students, perusing primary sources and pursuing independent research. The merger required a complex integration process and led to the macro-arrangement of books that persists today, with particular portions of the Library of Congress classification system assembled on designated floors.

Within that infrastructure, the number of books housed in the Hesburgh Library has kept on climbing. The building designed to hold at least two million books now holds many more than that, thanks largely to the installation of compact, movable shelving in the basement—the only floor strong enough to carry all that weight. The building's contents have expanded out across the university to constitute eight specialized libraries, resource centers, and reading rooms around campus under the umbrella title of the Hesburgh Libraries.

An exact quantity of books to be found in the flagship Hesburgh Library itself is both an elusive number and a moving target; the number of books owned by Notre Dame grows all the time. As of fiscal 2012, the Hesburgh Libraries (not including the Kresge Law Library or the University Archives) laid claim to about 3.9 million volumes, including electronic books. According to the statistics defined by the ARL, the Libraries also held approximately 60,000 serials (electronic and print), more than 2 million microform units, and 14,000 film and video materials, says Kelly McNally, executive administrator for Hesburgh Libraries.

Today's premier, state-of-the-art format, of course, is digital. It epitomizes the macro-trends that have changed libraries, learning, and the world—computerization and an information explosion that was only partially envisioned at Notre Dame's 1964 "Symposium on the Person in the Contemporary World." Computing was indeed part of the vision for the Memorial Library from its early days, as presaged by its proximity to the Univac 1107 computer, which occupied a large part of the Library's neighbor building, now called the Information Technology Center. One of the Library's occupants, a center for the study of artificial intelligence, further proved the musical maxim that Notre Dame "can't stop thinking about tomorrow."

But computers remained largely "behind the scenes" until the 1980s, when they became part of every patron's direct experience of the Library. Updating of the card catalog in its paper form ceased in 1987 as nearly everybody's searches moved online. When the card catalog furniture

Chapters of Change

was removed in 2001, librarians had been acquiring digital versions to replace or supplement hard-copy collections for more than a decade.

The new millennium buffeted the Library with a perfect storm of changing conditions. Notre Dame, elevating even further its aspiration to be among the leaders among U.S. research universities, attracted more professors and graduate students from elite institutions where top-shelf libraries, containing the best of everything, were expected as a given. Also, people demanded more information in digital form, accessible anywhere through ubiquitous Internet services. Publishers of academic journals and other materials found that they could provide formerly paper materials as digital products at high prices, often requiring costly annual subscriptions. The growth of e-journals, databases, and other online or CD-based tools required more people and more specialized skills to manage the abundance of new information, and to help patrons access them. Yet, in this world of computer "convenience" that fostered greater productivity and faster-paced lifestyles, many patrons felt less need to go physically to the library—and perhaps they had less time, or willingness, to make the trip.

At the same time, among other users, there was still a growing demand for books—more books about more topics, especially in the arts, humanities, and liberal arts. Demand particularly grew in fields where Notre Dame was increasing its engagement or becoming more global and interdisciplinary in its perspectives. The university and its peer institutions encouraged greater collaboration between the sciences and a spectrum of other disciplines to address the world's most urgent challenges. Of course, all the collaborators needing books on those subjects believed they needed them right away. On top of that, the U.S. dollar's weakness took its toll by making the purchase of books from Europe more expensive. And the slow growth in both the U.S. economy and the libraries' budget during much of the past decade made it challenging even to keep pace with growing demand.

The squeeze on Notre Dame's libraries became apparent in various ways. As reported by John Nagy in *Notre Dame Magazine* in the winter of 2009–2010, "The shelves in the Hesburgh Library are getting tight, but not fast enough, according to a faculty petition hand-delivered to the Dome by the chairs of the history and theology departments." A parallel petition from Notre Dame students made the same request for "a radical increase" in spending on acquisitions, as well as on research staff, renovations, and new storage space for lesser-used materials. Graduate student David Morris was quoted as saying Notre Dame "has not yet made the transition from a curriculum library to a research library." Morris, citing statistics from the Association of Research Libraries, argued: "If it is unacceptable for Notre Dame to be 56th in the *U.S. News* rankings, or 56th in the college football polls, it should also be unacceptable for Notre Dame—one of the world's wealthiest universities and champions of the Catholic intellectual tradition—to have a library that ranks 56th in the country."

The revolution of rising expectations prompted major adjustments during the first decade of the twenty-first century. Notions of self-sufficiency were replaced, or rather were complemented, by a readiness to share strengths. The libraries took a dual approach to providing resources, emphasizing a combination called "just in case" and "just in time." Under the first category, librarians continued aggressively to purchase complete menus of books—and digital materials—in fields where patron demand and University aspirations for growth were highest. The goal was to maximize the chance that even a seldom requested volume would be available "just in case" a pioneering scholar needed it. Under the second category, the aim was to obtain whatever scholars and students needed "just in time," even if the book or digital product was not immediately on hand. In the case of books, some little-used volumes that were housed in another library or storage space could still be obtained and delivered promptly to the patron. Similarly, the libraries need not subscribe to every print and e-journal in existence because sometimes a single article from a rarely used publication can simply be purchased on a one-time basis, as needed.

Tight squeezes and rapid changes that have occurred throughout the world of information science in recent years are seen in the reassessment of how to rank libraries, says Diane Parr Walker, who has been Notre Dame's Edward H. Arnold University Librarian since 2011. For decades, the rankings were largely based on the number of volumes a library held. The Association of Research Libraries (ARL) has realized that sheer quantity is not a complete measure of library success, especially in an age when so much information can easily be shared among libraries and among patrons.

"They're working on how to realistically assess the quality of a research library," Walker says of the ARL. Metrics now being used have more to do with a university's investment of dollars and human resources than they do with book-count. But even that measurement of inputs enjoyed by a library ultimately needs to be coupled with measurement of outcomes achieved by the library, she points out: "What is the contribution a library makes to the work of a university?" The bottom-line question is: How is the library helping to further the goals of the university and its academic community?

Walker points out that the metrics now being used—based on a formula that includes and weights a number of variables, including total library expenditures, total employees, and salaries for professional staff—rank Notre Dame in forty-ninth place. That spot in the ARL's Library Investment Index covering fiscal year 2009–2010 shows gains from the ranking cited in the graduate student's critique in *Notre Dame Magazine*.

Metrics for libraries' most meaningful accomplishments still need to be developed, but the Hesburgh Libraries are already prepared in that they are no stranger to the question of outcomes. The focus on achieving Notre Dame's purpose and mission was clear in Victor Schaefer's aforementioned 1959 planning memo: "The primary characteristic of a good academic library is its complete identification with its own institution," he wrote; "the measure of a library's excellence is the extent to which its services and resources support the institution's objectives and promote student and faculty achievement."

Father Ted and the Notre Dame family connected the Library to broader goals right from the start in 1958, in the "Program for the Future" capital campaign. Given the university's desire to make a difference in the modern world, to be (and to reflect) a source of light and hope for the human race, and to bring to bear the fullness of knowledge in pursuing the fullness of truth, Father Ted had rock-solid confidence in the towering contribution the Library would make as the intellectual heart of the campus. Regardless of the exact metrics for taking its pulse, being tied to a place of zeal and excellence like Notre Dame inevitably gives the Library a strong heartbeat.

One more development might be mentioned in this review of macro-changes, especially when the discussion turns to matters of the heart. The Memorial Library's name-change to the

Hesburgh Library in 1987 was only the first recognition that the building owed its existence to Father Ted's passion for the university's mission and character.

In 2005, a sculpture was installed near the reflecting pool, sure to be seen by most of those seeking entry through the Library's main, south-facing doors and those wanting a close-up view of the *Word of Life* mural. The larger-than-life bronze sculpture, an idea birthed from the fiftieth reunion of Notre Dame's class of 1953, pictures Father Ted standing in conversation with his colleague, Father Ned Joyce. The class of '53 was the first class to graduate under the leadership of Fathers Ted and Ned. The class gift utilized the services of sculptor Lou Cella, who continues a successful career today, often called upon to immortalize famous sports figures.

The sculpture at the Hesburgh Library conveys messages from the hearts of both men. A quote from Father Ned at the base of the sculpture reads: "Notre Dame is first and foremost a university, and only insofar as it excels as a university can it give proper homage to the patroness who bears as one of her noble titles, Seat of Wisdom."

The accompanying quote from Father Ted goes even further in connecting the Library to the university's identity and suggesting how success might be measured: "A Catholic university should be a beacon, bringing to light, in modern focus, the wonderfully traditional and ancient adage, 'faith seeking understanding.' It should be a crossroads where all the intellectual and moral currents of our time meet and are truthfully considered."

In 2008, the University Libraries of Notre Dame were renamed the Hesburgh Libraries so as to unite all the specialized branches and reading rooms under a single "brand"—in this case, a time-tested vision and sense of purpose, and a great leader's knack for creating connections between people and ideas.

"Renaming the entire University Libraries system after Father Ted is an appropriate way to honor the depth and breadth of his vision for interdisciplinary excellence at Notre Dame," President Rev. John Jenkins, C.S.C., said at the time. "Now, the Hesburgh Libraries include not only the monument to learning called the Hesburgh Library but also the various subject-specific libraries that bring the world-class resources and expertise to faculty and students all around campus."

INNOVATIONS AND RENOVATIONS

Because Notre Dame and the Hesburgh Library seek truth among all things visible and invisible, the preceding journey through fifty years in terms of macro-trends and ideas should now give way to a review of changes obvious to the naked eye. The world of information has been advancing without pause through the decades, and the university has worked hard to keep pace, indeed to be a pace-setter, often in ways behind the scenes or in the realm of ideas. But as we are living in a material world, our tour can pause at a few key physical milestones to savor the view.

One perfect place to capture a snapshot in time is the Clarke Memorial Fountain, which was built in 1985 on the former site of Notre Dame's classic Field House, to the west of the Library. The stately fountain, featuring limestone columns that rise from a granite pool and surround a granite sphere, honors university alumni who have served in World War II and in military conflicts since that time. Named after its principal donor, Maude Clarke, the fountain was designed by John Burgee with his partner Philip Johnson. Burgee is a 1956 Notre Dame graduate, nationally renowned architect, and now a Notre Dame Trustee Emeritus. The fountain has its own student nickname—Stonehenge—and has connections to the Hesburgh Library more as a medium than as a message. With the removal of the Field House as a dominant physical separator between the Library and the main "God Quad," circumstances seemed to reassert the three-in-one skyline vision of Father Ted, where Library, Basilica, and Golden Dome are of a piece.

A straight line leads from the Library to the Basilica, whose eastern door has special meaning as a memorial to alumni who served in World War I. Over that door are inscribed the enduring words, "God, Country, Notre Dame."

Burgee picks up the story from there: "Father Ted had for a long time wanted to honor the Notre Dame grads that served in wars since World War I. When he first talked to me about the memorial, it was not a very popular time with the students to build anything that might look like honoring war. . . . He felt that a fountain would be a beautiful attribute for the campus and would not be an objectionable memorial—especially if dedicated to peace, which, after all, was what these men were fighting for. It was known then as the Clarke Peace Fountain."

Burgee continues: "When I started work [on the fountain], a site for it had been selected adjacent to Breen Philips Hall. When studying the plan, however, it became clear that the axis from the Library to the Basilica was where it belonged, and Father Ted agreed. I was very much aware of the Library's terminal position on the east-west quad axis with the World War I memorial door, but this axis needed reinforcing. I felt that the intersection with the North Quad was critical and required a strong element marking this intersection. It would be the focus and turning point of the two quads—a prominent and honorable position for such an important monument."

This was the genesis for a threefold procession of memorials—from Basilica to fountain to Library—and an orderly grid of open spaces well-suited to open minds. The connections did not stop there, however, because one more visual tie-in materialized. Observers appreciating the proud, strong pillars of the fountain from a viewpoint to the west cannot help but notice that the fountain's rectangular design is a virtually perfect, proportional fit within the design of the Library's tower and penthouse.

"While I was aware of the Library and needed to be compatible with it, I did not consciously echo the Library form or structure," says Burgee. One might summarize that the fountain was not designed to mimic the Library, but both its design and location were adapted to fit in well with the Library and indeed with all its surroundings.

"The geometry of the fountain comfortably fits its location and is a wonderful place on campus that draws many people," says University Architect Douglas Marsh. Notre Dame always approaches its architectural planning from the perspective of the whole—ensuring that the design and placement of any new element take into account the network of quads and grids that unifies the campus. Marsh compares the planning of any new construction to "welcoming another member of the family." He says orderly patterns and open spaces are important in planning: "We're about building a beautiful campus, not individual buildings."

In this way, the addition of the Clarke Memorial Fountain reaffirmed the philosophy that had guided the placement of the Library itself, a philosophy that encourages people to explore connections and crossroads even as they enjoy a sense of good order, whether consciously or subconsciously. Perhaps no one has evinced this constancy-plus-change approach as a way of life more than Father Ted, so the fountain was a providential gift, anticipating by a few years the unified, harmonized view that Father Ted would see through the west-facing window as he gazed toward the Basilica and Our Lady on the dome. Regarding the fountain itself, Burgee recalls, "The students accepted it wholeheartedly, and it became a favorite meeting place. It also became a great pleasure for Father Ted, as he could see it from his office in the Library."

Respecting the patterns of the past is important at Notre Dame, but so is moving forward. In that latter spirit, there have been a number of material changes made at the Library itself, serving as preludes to further renovation and foreshadowings of the future.

140

In 1994, the university gave the thirty-year-old *Word of Life* mural a $280,000 facelift. Conrad Schmitt Studios, based in New Berlin, Wisconsin, replaced some of the panels and gold leaf, and did some recaulking. This was the same firm that regilded the Golden Dome in 1988 and 2005.

A team of workers took to the scaffolds during the summer of 2011 to perform more extensive maintenance work on the mural. This time, they replaced the urethane adhesive holding the mural to the building, applying a more water-resistant elastomeric sealant. They made extensive repairs to the building's masonry, cleaning out and replacing joints that had suffered from decades of freeze-thaw cycles, according to Marsh. They touched up spots of worn paint and gold leaf. All building surfaces were washed with a light detergent.

To do justice to the brighter colors and sharper definition of the mural—and for the sake of sustainability—the university replaced mercury vapor lamps with more energy-efficient LED (light-emitting diode) lights to illuminate the mural. The LED lights are brighter and save approximately 57,000 kilowatt hours of electricity annually. "The replacement has also improved the nighttime appearance of the mural twofold," the university reported. "Because of the mercury contained in the old lights, the mural previously appeared to have a green tint. The LED lights make the mural brighter, and the stones of the mosaic appear more natural. Furthermore, these new lights have been engineered to only shine light to the top of the mural, therefore preventing excess sky glow and allowing for a better view of the stars."

The new lighting system also allows for more versatility and creativity, says Marsh. During the annual "Notre Dame Relay for Life: Fighting Irish Fighting Cancer" event in 2012, the university placed purple lenses on the mural lights to recognize the event's official color, sending symbolic support to the participants in the nighttime event. Additional splashes of assorted colors are likely at future events.

The massive renovations completed in 2011 on the exterior of the building also included a regilding of the "symbols of Christ" engravings that now jump out more boldly to pedestrians from the granite walls of the first floor.

Just as the university paved the way for the Library's future by refreshing the most visible and venerable part of the building, the new millennium brought renovation plans for the interior, too. A gift of more than $16 million from the estate of the late William J. Carey '46—which in 2000 was the largest estate gift ever made to the University—went in part to support the planning of a long-term renovation project. The auditorium on the Library's main floor was renovated and renamed the William J. Carey Auditorium.

The first phase of the broader reconstruction started in early 2002 and focused on the lower level, where "the maze of blank corridors and windowless offices" was replaced with an assortment of dark wood booths, tables, and study spaces, as *Notre Dame Magazine* reported upon completion of the project in autumn 2003. Many of those offices had been vacant for a long time, since faculty members and academic offices had moved to Decio Hall and other locations. "Gone are the Formica booths and vending machines of 'the Pit' snack area." The space has become a popular destination for students intent upon quiet study. The remodeling also opened up abundant space for special collections and for storage of other books in modern compact shelving.

Renovation of the penthouse followed in 2004–2005, and changes were made to the first floor layout in 2007–2009. The Reference Services Department was renamed Information, Research, and Instructional Services, or IRIS, and was given a new, computerized home where students and faculty could visit a "hub" of services to meet their research needs. "Collaboration stations" were added close-by, ready to accommodate various configurations of students with their laptops and books.

Those steps proved to be only the beginning of a transformation on the first floor. In the summer of 2012, the large space that had served as the periodicals reading room became a brighter, more colorful, hybrid space symbolizing the Library's new era of innovation and adaptation. Different sections of the room, affectionately dubbed the "fishbowl" because of its glass walls, became spaces for student collaborations, relaxed individual study, lectures and presentations, and a "technology sandbox," all outfitted with different kinds of tables and chairs. One planned high-tech feature was a sixteen-panel "video wall," four square feet in dimension, suited to large digital images, bound to create a sense of excitement and curiosity among passersby in the concourse.

The stated goal is to create "a welcoming and flexible space" that will support a range of intellectual activities and experiences that will help librarians and those they serve imagine the future of the whole Library.

Speaking of a welcoming space, the other major change on the main floor in 2012 was the opening of a Library café for light dining and conversation. An "Au Bon Pain" franchise took over space that previously had been filled with vending machines from the lower level's prerenovation era. The new space looks out onto the beautifully remodeled Richard and Mary Carey Courtyard at the southern main entrance of the building, with plenty of seating around abundant trees, part of a popular new gathering space—or crossroads—for the campus community. The trees and their planters help to make a cooler, more human-scale space than the previous space above which the hot sun shone and the *Word of Life* mural soared.

The material used in building the walls of the six giant planters represents connectedness with the rest of campus. University Architect Marsh points out that the new seating walls are made with Cold Spring Granite, from Minnesota, returning to one of the original building materials of the Library. The pink-tinted granite is in use in many places on campus—in the equally low structures that constitute the walls of remembrance around the reflecting pool, in the base of Alumni and Dillon Halls, and in the base of the much newer Eck Hall of Law. It is also in the

gateway entrance to campus on Notre Dame Avenue and in the Founders Wall that honors major benefactors near the entrance to Irish Green.

MORE CHANGES ON MANY LEVELS

Just as the structures of the Library are now in the process of harmonizing with the past and future of the University, the interior spaces and everyday activities of the building must continue to adapt to the rapid changes in the world of information.

As university librarian, Diane Parr Walker is leading the Hesburgh Library's foray into the future in the spirit of continuity with the past. The basic mission is largely unchanged, even though the shift away from books and toward digital media in recent years prompted some to wonder whether libraries were becoming obsolete.

"We are getting past those questions now," says Walker. "We understand better what the digital age will offer." As with the birth of other media in the past, like radio and television, new conduits of information seldom replace their predecessors completely. Instead, they merge in some ways and distinguish themselves in other ways. Connecting people to knowledge matters more than the means by which it is accomplished.

"Libraries were never exclusively about books," says Walker. "They were always about intellectual connectedness, about being an intellectual crossroads." Libraries will never be obsolete because that intellectual intersection is more bustling than ever before. What's happening at the crossroads?

Interdisciplinary knowledge—along with the pursuit of it—is growing, she points out. At a time when universities are planning more places where "interdisciplinarity" is nurtured, "libraries are the original multidisciplinary research building."

Research is booming in general, especially at Notre Dame. As quoted in the *NDWorks* faculty-staff newspaper in 2012, Provost Thomas G. Burish has said, "Responding to the many demands and challenges of supporting our vision of being the pre-eminent Catholic research university will require a forward-looking University library system that is prepared to meet the future research, scholarship, and teaching needs of faculty and students."

The Hesburgh Libraries have been looking ahead by investing more aggressively in the components of a superior research library—strong additions to print and digital collections, plus increases to in-house expertise in particular academic disciplines, as well as in technology. The mantra of "service excellence" has been promulgated throughout the libraries, and the faculty and staff have been reorganized. Even as individuals' jobs have become more multifaceted, demanding additional skill sets, employees are focusing on how their own roles fit together as part of a team in the service to students and professors, to learning and teaching.

Walker also wants that sense of teamwork to grow between library faculty and the university's research and teaching faculty. "We're aiming to be collaborators, to be seen as partners with faculty members and students around the campus in their research endeavors." As library subject experts work closely with academic departments and colleges, they can make sure their plans and priorities are in sync so that resources will be on hand to meet growing needs, and resources won't be wasted in areas where the emphasis is shrinking or shifting.

The combination of better on-campus coordination to anticipate future research needs and better coordination among librarians (on- and off-campus) to make sure all resources can be shared efficiently means that the "just in case" approach to buying books can become a better fit with the "just in time" criterion. Plentiful book purchases will continue into the future, says Walker, particularly in core collections and in the "print intensive" disciplines of the arts, humanities, and liberal arts, but better planning can largely eliminate the inefficiency of trying to predict potential demands and buying books unlikely to be used. Anyway, research libraries are working harder to make sure that those less frequently used books will always be stored somewhere, without needless duplication, and quickly delivered as needed—in print form, upon faculty or student request—when instant digital access isn't possible.

All fields of study, even the more print-intensive ones, are making rich use of digital information, and it's a library's job to help that use to grow, Walker says.

Computing is "a force multiplier for learning," substantially boosting the potential for the quantity, quality, and impact of learning in all fields, from science to the humanities. Students and their professor in a history course can now imagine how information found in a book or map could be combined not only with other printed materials, but with historical and current (perhaps real-time) details, and displayed visually to a whole class for comparative analysis. Librarians have always been "a kind of sherpa" guiding people through a maze of information. Increasingly, the right team of library professionals will help a "digital humanities" class not only

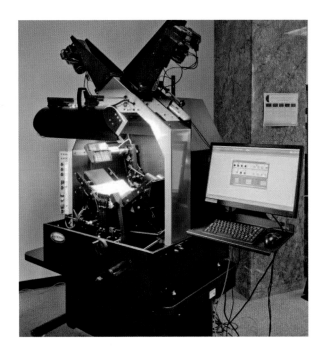

find the print material to use as a springboard, but also suggest the kinds of digital tools that might uncover additional insights, and then make the technology available for overlaying and visualizing that information in a convenient workspace.

Data constitutes a new kind of treasure, different from and yet comparable to the varied kinds of treasures traditionally embraced by the Hesburgh Libraries and described earlier in this book, such as special collections, an array of "realia," and real people such as students, faculty, library professionals, and benefactors. The notion of "data curation" is akin to the work of all curators—preserving, "mining," and providing data, making it accessible and usable, appreciating and enhancing its value. "Text-mining" is emerging as a resource for analysis of entire books or large numbers of books (or other texts, like social media); finding patterns and gaining new insights into the words people used and the thoughts they expressed—using language like any other data—can help interpret, predict, and create knowledge. The possibilities for building new discoveries upon existing data are naturally exciting in fields such as the sciences, engineering, and the social sciences, but new perspectives and innovative ideas arise in every field and will be able to draw upon swift currents of data like never before—with help from skilled navigators.

Importantly, all the different kinds of treasures will remain on-site and on the Library's collective mind. Curators and other knowledge leaders will work together, partly to maximize the synergies between different technologies and forms of information. For example, special collections—from medieval manuscripts to sports research collections to Latin American literature—will remain very important in the Hesburgh Libraries. The Library will add to the existing collections and build new collections responsive to growing interests of the university.

All of this growth can take both print and digital forms, Walker says. As of 2012, the Library was working closely with the Institute for Latino Studies to build onto the university's already formidable resources related to Latin America in a way that also serves research needs (historical and up-to-the-minute) about Latinos in the United States.

Separately, a new special collection was taking shape thanks to teamwork with the Nanovic Institute for European Studies. Semion Lyandres, co-director of the Program in Russian and Eastern European Studies, made it possible for the libraries to acquire valuable print transcriptions of oral history interviews with individuals who had been involved in the Russian Revolution of 1917. Other oral histories relevant to that period were obtained in digital form.

"It's a fabulous treasure trove for historians," says Walker. Rare and unique collections will always be a vital part of the Hesburgh Libraries. Indeed, in this age when more and more information can be shared across the Internet or through "interlibrary loan" systems, collections of material that serve a particular university's priority research areas, or represent a special coordination with the university's leaders and mission, will help to keep each library unique and especially attuned to its home institution.

At the same time, there will be subjects of shared interest that unite librarians and academic leaders across distances and disciplines. As the guarantors of access to today's knowledge, university libraries are among those at the center of debates about intellectual property, academic freedom, privacy, government censorship or corporate controls, and information gaps between different segments of society. All these questions of access have become more complicated and urgent in the digital age.

As of 2012, the University of Notre Dame was one of more than sixty individual institutional members in the HathiTrust, a partnership dedicated to "collecting, organizing, preserving, communicating, and sharing the record of human knowledge." Among other goals, this entails establishing "a reliable and increasingly comprehensive digital archive of library materials converted from print that is co-owned and managed by a number of academic institutions," as the HathiTrust says on its website. *NDWorks* reported in 2012 that the Hesburgh Libraries and dozens of HathiTrust partners had "contributed more than 10 million volumes" to their digital archive. The word "Hathi" is Hindi for "elephant," the animal that symbolizes a long memory.

The HathiTrust itself symbolizes the triumphs and tensions of building a worldwide storehouse of knowledge. Much more information can now be shared instantly and electronically, so there is less need for each individual institution to have a comprehensive collection in-house. This is great progress, but the systems and protocols for sharing require constant coordination, making it a good thing that library faculty are accountable not only for the smooth functioning of their own internal operations, but also for collaboration in their broader profession of information science. These professionals' diligence must span multiple institutions and encompass all the broad, evolving issues of common concern. The existence of professional standards and influence can be a bulwark against inadequate or improper stewardship of information by corporations, governments, and individuals.

What implications do all these trends have for the Hesburgh Library? To some degree, the answer to that question will continue to evolve along with the information age. But the university's plans are clear on some key points, including appropriate physical changes.

The renovations accomplished so far on the entire exterior and on the interior of the lower level and the first floor are only the beginning, says Walker: "Next is a plan to renovate the interior of the entire building." As of 2012, the university was developing a master plan envisioning various kinds of spaces that should be created for various purposes "and then determining how to use the square footage we have to create those various spaces." The different areas established in the

first-floor "fishbowl" were experimental, in a way, to see what features attracted the greatest use and the kinds of comfortable, even inspiring, spaces for which visitors were still looking.

One thing is clear. The Hesburgh Library comprises 430,000 square feet of prime real estate on campus—and books must share that space with other uses. As of 2012, the search was on for suitable locations where perhaps a third of the building's physical volumes could be stored for easy retrieval and quick delivery. Separate shelving facilities would open up much of the second floor and tower for new layouts.

The new designs could include more space for group study and collaborative efforts, reflecting the fact that many students are less inclined toward independent work in the library than they used to be. These could be areas combining print and digital resources devoted to a single subject or related subjects, especially respecting the needs of print-intensive disciplines. Starting in the fall of 2013, the Hesburgh Library will be home to the Center for Digital Scholarship. Available for use by students and faculty members, complete with easy access to technology and expertise—both technical and discipline-specific—that will facilitate classes and other scholarly pursuits in a digital mode.

A reduced emphasis on book storage in the Hesburgh Library will mean an increased presence of digital storage, which requires less physical space but substantial financial investments in technology and human expertise, says Walker. Plenty of space will still be dedicated to the growth in and use of special collections—along with all materials (in multiple forms) especially well-suited to Notre Dame research priorities.

The Library (along with all the units of the Hesburgh Libraries system) will still be places of preservation, where books linking the university and its scholarship to the past as well as the future will be stored and cared for—and made quickly available. It will be a place where people can go to consult with each other, to study together, to brainstorm around smart tables, and to consume masses of information visually and vividly. But it will also have spaces where people can go for quiet study or reflection. Some librarians are even proposing technology-free zones, where the human mind and heart can find respite with each other. Father Ted's solicitude for the human person as an ultimate treasure to be protected and celebrated throughout any information explosion would seem to require some room for sharing peace.

STILL TRUE TO ITS WORD

In short, the Hesburgh Library of the future will be a collection of many spaces and roles, all of them valuable for various people and endeavors—and thus meaningful to the entire Notre Dame community, and beyond.

"It doesn't belong to any one discipline," Walker says of the Library. "It belongs to all of them. And therefore it can serve as the kind of intellectual crossroads that brings a lot of different people and resources and academic pursuits together—and allows for the creation of new understanding and new knowledge."

The meaning of the building thus holds true to the message of its mural. Millard Sheets's portrayal of Christ the Teacher, upholding truth as the goal in the search for knowledge and positing a purpose for always aiming higher, speaks boldly today to scholars, students, and visitors alike. For many at Notre Dame, the theme of Christ the Teacher helps to sum up what has brought them to the campus. The words of scripture that invoke the Word of Life—particularly the beginning of the First Epistle of John and the start of John's Gospel—fit well with the mission of

Chapters of Change

engaging people in lively dialogue, a process of avid teaching and learning that enhances freedom and promotes justice.

The Alliance for Catholic Education (ACE), for instance, which sends forth graduate students and teams of education experts "to serve, sustain, and transform Catholic schools," sees Christ the Teacher as a primary model. Celebrating its own twentieth anniversary in 2013–2014, ACE is one key example of the Congregation of Holy Cross commitment to make God known, loved, and served. Similar examples abound across campus in which resources are marshaled to meet needs in a spirit of service and love.

Sheets's *Word of Life* mural, made with the enduring strength of granite to adorn a tower that Father Ted raised by the sheer force of his vision and zeal, stands as a symbol of joyful hope.

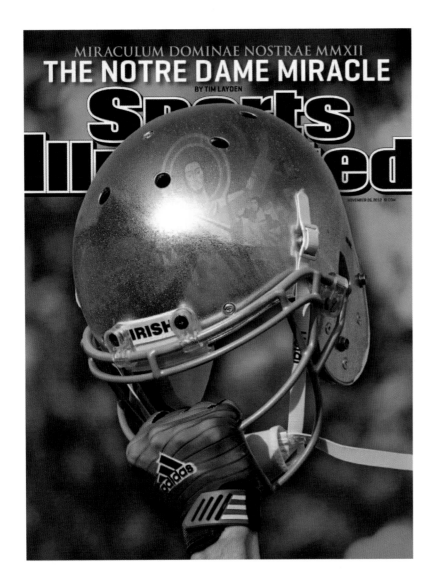
MIRACULUM DOMINAE NOSTRAE MMXII
THE NOTRE DAME MIRACLE
BY TIM LAYDEN
Sports Illustrated
IRISH
NOVEMBER 26, 2012 SI.COM

Sports Illustrated affirmed this with its November 26, 2012, cover image marking the Fighting Irish 12-0 season—an image in which the mural was reflected in a football player's raised helmet. The image evokes not only present success, but also the enduring traditions of the university. The echoes of the past continue to resonate today.

University Architect Doug Marsh asserts that the Hesburgh Library still has plenty of life in it. Indeed, the Library is almost exactly at the mean in terms of the life spans of campus buildings. It is neither young nor old: "The average age of a square foot on campus dates to 1963." He says there's every reason to expect that, with his office's usual vigilance and maintenance, all the buildings can stand tall in perpetuity.

Walker confirms that the Hesburgh Library is a valuable, centrally located gem, already reasserting itself as a place of creativity and connectivity. Multimedia technology is making it better than ever as a staging area for synergies between the material treasures (like special collections, manuscripts, and today's manifold expressions of information) and the human treasures (like benefactors, librarians, learners, and leaders). It's much more than a building. It is increasingly inseparable from an array of information resources, local and global; it is better understood today as a reflection of people, ideas, and values in motion. Even if libraries in general risk becoming interchangeable, sharing resources and channeling information through the same devices, the Hesburgh Library will always be distinctive and dynamic as "a Notre Dame place."

The courtyard at the building's entrance is now more bustling and inviting, and it opens onto a Library Quad that has been an exciting gathering place from its formation. In 1964, it hosted a Pontifical Mass. In 2011, it hosted a Mass marking the tenth anniversary of the 9/11 tragedy. In 2012, it hosted the ESPN College GameDay show—and a huge crowd of fans celebrating the University's enduring athletic excellence.

Over the years, the Library and those associated with it have taken their share of criticism—for its shape and size, for its internal and external aesthetics (including its mural), for the quality and quantity of its collections, and for its adaptations to the changing information world. The criticisms reflect one perception of Notre Dame itself: a "most recognizable (and polarizing) brand," as Jason Gay of the *Wall Street Journal* described the football program in a November 27, 2012, article. Undeterred by disagreements, the Notre Dame family will continue to invest emotions and more into this remarkable campus asset. It exists to help achieve the university's strategic plans and highest aspirations, and it preserves a distinctive collection of treasures tailored over time to the university's special loves and loyalties. It will continue to remind a worldwide audience that there's no place like Notre Dame.

And that place called Notre Dame continues to grow its prominence as a Catholic research university, confronting urgent challenges in the sciences and many other fields with its interdisciplinary instincts. The Library was built for such times as these. It dates back to a period when the questions were similar, to a decade when perceptions of rapid and massive change stirred fears but also suggested new possibilities for humanity. Today, it stands proudly with the whole university, taking a purposeful, open-minded, never-say-die approach to the most daunting challenges.

As the Library begins its next fifty years, it especially resonates with the words of Father Ted, who envisioned a treasure house for knowledge and a dynamic place for free inquiry—but no room for pessimism. As cited earlier in this book, he told benefactors in the early 1960s: "I don't mean that Notre Dame is going to solve all the world's problems, but I am convinced that many of our students who pass through the doors of this Library are going to comprehend better just what the whole world is today, and what it needs."

The words of life, in all their forms, remain on hand at Notre Dame as tools to be used wisely—sure to be accessed, embraced, and utilized in ways that can barely be imagined today. Those countless, powerful entry points to understanding, in the hands of a good teacher, will support the discernment of answers, always renewing the university's hopeful vision for the twenty-first century. It will take a lot of good people to make every word count, and the Hesburgh Library endures as a place of meaningful perspective from which that endeavor proceeds.

Photo Credits

49   Transporting of books from Lemmonier Library to Memorial Library via conveyor belt and beer cartons. Courtesy of the University of Notre Dame Archives.

50   Library construction "topping out" ceremony. Rev. Theodore Hesburgh signing an I-beam. April 3, 1962. Courtesy of the University of Notre Dame Archives.

51   Library, exterior view without the *Word of Life* mural, ca. 1963. Courtesy of the University of Notre Dame Archives.

Chapter Two

52   *Word of Life* mural. Photo by Matt Cashore.

54   Central Library at the Universidad Nacional Autónoma de México (UNAM) in Mexico City. From the Hal Box and Logan Wagner Collection of Mexican Architecture and Urban Design. Image courtesy of the School of Architecture Visual Resources Collection, University of Texas at Austin.

55   Millard Sheets mural sketch, ca. 1960s. Courtesy of the University of Notre Dame Archives.

56   A portion of the full-size rendering of the *Word of Life* mural in a gymnasium in Cold Spring, Minnesota. Courtesy of and copyright 2013 Coldspring (formerly the Cold Spring Granite Company).

57   Millard Sheets with the full-size "cartoon" of the *Word of Life* mural. Susan Lautman Hertel, his assistant for forty years, is sitting on the scaffold to the upper left. Courtesy of Tony Sheets.

58   Design work on *Word of Life* mural, ca. 1962. Pictured individual identified by *American Artist* magazine as Millard Sheets. Courtesy of the University of Notre Dame Archives.

59   Cold Spring employee fitting pieces of mural at fabrication facility. Courtesy of and copyright 2013 Coldspring (formerly the Cold Spring Granite Company).

61   Details of the *Word of Life* mural. Photo by Matt Cashore

62   Mural assembly. Courtesy of AECOM.

63   Mural detail. Courtesy of AECOM.

65   Mural assembly. Courtesy of AECOM.

66   *Word of Life* mural, installation of the head of Christ, ca. 1964. Courtesy of the University of Notre Dame Archives.

68   *Word of Life* mural, ca. 1990s. Photo by Matt Cashore.

69   Scaffolding for library mural. Courtesy of Ellerbe Becket/AECOM.

71   Display of endowed professorships along the library reflecting pool wall. Photo by Matt Cashore.

73   Library mural informational plaque, ca. 1964. Courtesy of the University of Notre Dame Archives.

74   Close-up of the face of Jesus from the *Word of Life* mural. Photo by Matt Cashore.

77–78   The Symbols of Christ on the outside wall of the Library. Photo by Matt Cashore.

79   Model of Moses statue by Joseph Turkalj, 1963. Courtesy of the University of Notre Dame Archives.

80   (*left*) Three clay models of Moses. Courtesy AECOM.
     (*right*) Joseph Turkalj working on Moses statue, 1963. Courtesy of the University of Notre Dame Archives.

81   Joseph Turkalj working on Moses statue, 1963. Courtesy of the University of Notre Dame Archives.

82   Moses sculpture by Ivan Mestrovic, on display on second floor of the Library. Photo by Matt Cashore.

83   Moses statue and "burning bush" outside the Library. Photo by Matt Cashore.

86–87   Library renovations, the "fishbowl." Photo by Matt Cashore.

88   Library interior, first floor. Copyright University of Notre Dame.

Chapter Three

90   St. Patrick stained glass window in the Special Collections reading room in the Library. Photo by Matt Cashore.

92–93   Library basement interiors after renovation in 2002–3. Copyright University of Notre Dame.

95   Snack and vending machine area on the first floor of the Library before renovations in 2012. Photo by Matt Cashore

97   Medieval Institute, seventh floor of the Library. Photo by Matt Cashore.

99   Library interior, second floor. Copyright University of Notre Dame.

100   The graduate student lounge on the tenth floor of the Library. Photo by Matt Cashore.